ASTON VILLA
CHAMPIONS
1980/81

ASTON VILLA CHAMPIONS

1980/81

John Shipley

TEMPUS

This book is dedicated to my wife Kate.

Frontispiece: Aston Villa's 1895 FA Cup-winning team.

First published 2005

Tempus Publishing Limited
The Mill, Brimscombe Port,
Stroud, Gloucestershire, GL5 2QG
www.tempus-publishing.com

© John Shipley, 2005

The right of John Shipley to be identified as the Author
of this work has been asserted in accordance with the
Copyrights, Designs and Patents Act 1988.

British Library Cataloguing in Publication Data.
A catalogue record for this book is available from the British Library.

ISBN 0 7524 3610 4

Typesetting and origination by Tempus Publishing Limited.
Printed in Great Britain.

Acknowledgements

I would like to say a big thank you to the following people for the assistance they have given to me during the production of this book, in particular to everyone at Tempus Publishing. An extra-special thank you goes to Aston Villa Football Club for winning all those lovely trophies, and to everyone who has helped me with information, or has loaned Aston Villa memorabilia, in particular to Ray Whitehouse, Nick Bond and Mel Eves. Thanks also to Rob Stanway, Barry Carver and Michael Hewitt. A huge thank you goes to my long-suffering proofreading text-typing wife Kate. My thanks also go to the following: The *Birmingham Post & Mail*, the *Sports Argus*, the *Sunday Mercury*, the staff at the Birmingham City Library, Archives and Local Studies service, the staff at the Wolverhampton Archives and Local Studies service, the *Express & Star*.

Photographic and other acknowledgements: while every effort has been made to trace and acknowledge all copyright holders, we apologise for any errors or omissions. The author wishes to thank and acknowledge the following for providing photographs and for permission to reproduce copyright material: Empics photographic library service, the staff at the Birmingham City Library, Archives and Local Studies service, Ben Smallman, Mel Eves.

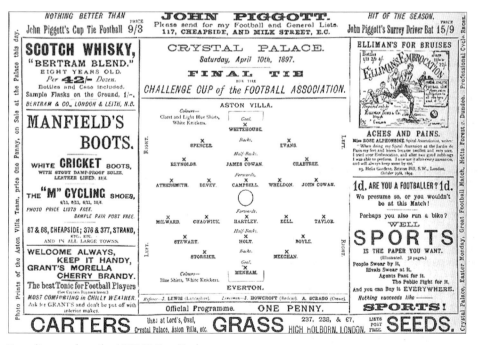

Team line-ups from the 1897 FA Cup Final.

List of Matches

All games are Football League unless otherwise stated.

Saturday 16 August 1980   Leeds United 1 Aston Villa 2

Wednesday 20 August 1980   Aston Villa 1 Norwich City 0

Saturday 23 August 1980   Manchester City 2 Aston Villa 2

Wednesday 27 August 1980   Aston Villa 1 Leeds United 0 (League Cup second round first leg)

Saturday 30 August 1980   Aston Villa 1 Coventry City 0

Wednesday 3 September 1980   Leeds United 1 Aston Villa 3 (League Cup second round second leg)

Saturday 6 September 1980   Ipswich Town 1 Aston Villa 0

Saturday 13 September 1980   Aston Villa 0 Everton 2

Saturday 20 September 1980   Aston Villa 2 Wolverhampton Wanderers 1

Tuesday 23 September 1980   Cambridge United 2 Aston Villa 1 (League Cup third round)

Saturday 27 September 1980   Crystal Palace 0 Aston Villa 1

Saturday 4 October 1980   Aston Villa 4 Sunderland 0

Wednesday 8 October 1980   Manchester United 3 Aston Villa 3

Saturday 11 October 1980   Birmingham City 1 Aston Villa 2

Saturday 18 October 1980   Aston Villa 3 Tottenham Hotspur 0

Wednesday 22 October 1980   Aston Villa 4 Brighton & Hove Albion 1

Saturday 25 October 1980   Southampton 1 Aston Villa 2

Saturday 1 November 1980   Aston Villa 2 Leicester City 0

Saturday 8 November 1980   West Bromwich Albion 0 Aston Villa 0

Wednesday 12 November 1980 Norwich City 1 Aston Villa 3

Saturday 15 November 1980   Aston Villa 1 Leeds United 1

Saturday 22 November 1980   Liverpool 2 Aston Villa 1

Saturday 29 November 1980   Aston Villa 1 Arsenal 1

Saturday 6 December 1980	Middlesbrough 2 Aston Villa 1
Saturday 13 December 1980	Aston Villa 3 Birmingham City 0
Saturday 20 December 1980	Brighton & Hove Albion 1 Aston Villa 0
Friday 26 December 1980	Aston Villa 1 Stoke City 0
Saturday 27 December 1980	Nottingham Forest 2 Aston Villa 2
Saturday 3 January 1981	Ipswich Town 1 Aston Villa 0 (FA Cup third round)
Saturday 10 January 1981	Aston Villa 2 Liverpool 0
Saturday 17 January 1981	Coventry City 1 Aston Villa 2
Saturday 31 January 1981	Aston Villa 1 Manchester City 0
Saturday 7 February 1981	Everton 1 Aston Villa 3
Saturday 21 February 1981	Aston Villa 2 Crystal Palace 1
Saturday 28 February 1981	Wolverhampton Wanderers 0 Aston Villa 1
Saturday 7 March 1981	Sunderland 1 Aston Villa 2
Saturday 14 March 1981	Aston Villa 3 Manchester United 3
Saturday 21 March 1981	Tottenham Hotspur 2 Aston Villa 0
Saturday 28 March 1981	Aston Villa 2 Southampton 1
Saturday 4 April 1981	Leicester City 2 Aston Villa 4
Wednesday 8 April 1981	Aston Villa 1 West Bromwich Albion 0
Tuesday 14 April 1981	Aston Villa 1 Ipswich Town 2
Saturday 18 April 1981	Aston Villa 2 Nottingham Forest 0
Monday 20 April 1981	Stoke City 1 Aston Villa 1
Saturday 25 April 1981	Aston Villa 3 Middlesbrough 0
Saturday 2 May 1981	Arsenal 2 Aston Villa 0

Introduction

By the beginning of the twentieth century Aston Villa had already established a prominent place in the English football hall of fame, winning three FA Cups in 1886/87, 1894/95 and 1896/97 plus five league championships in 1893/94, 1895/96, 1896/97, 1898/99 and 1899/1900. In the inaugural season of the league, 1888/89, Aston Villa were runners-up to Double-winners Preston North End, and were FA Cup runners-up in 1891/92. Aston Villa continued to win trophies, notably the FA Cup in 1904/05, 1912/13 and 1919/20, and the league championship in 1909/10, but further trophy success eluded the club until 1956/57 when the FA Cup, Villa's seventh, was once again brought back to Aston. In the league, the fans had to wait over seventy years to repeat the feat of 1909/10 and win their seventh league title. This is the story of that tremendous achievement.

The club's origins took shape in the winter of 1873/74, when a bunch of enthusiastic cricketers at the Villa Cross Wesleyan chapel in Lozells Road, Aston, were looking for a sport to play during the winter months. They decided to form an association football team. They were humble men from ordinary backgrounds coming together to create a footballing dynasty packed with tradition, founded on the back of the values of good sportsmanship and the ideals of the true Corinthian spirit.

Aston Villa's 1897 FA Cup-winning squad.

There was a scarcity of football teams in the area in their first season of 1874/75. The club reputedly played their inaugural game, against Aston Park Unity in January 1875, on a strip of land in the old deer park of Aston Hall, then known as the Aston Upper Grounds. These days we know it as Aston Park. The game itself is shrouded in mystery with uncertainty about the playing rules, except that both teams fielded fourteen players and Villa lost. The Aston Villa team that day was: W. Scattergood, G. Matthews, W.H. Price, S. McBenn, W. Mason, A. Walters, E. Lee, J. Hughes, A. Robbins, W. Weiss, H. Matthews, T. Smith, C. Midgley and F. Lewis.

The club's second game took place in March 1875, against Aston Brook St Mary's rugby team. Their opponents agreed to the game on the basis that in the first half they played rugby, under rugby union rules, using an oval ball, and the second half they played football, under Sheffield association rules, using a round football. The venue was a field situated in Birchfields, where Wilson Road is today. In this somewhat bizarre game, both sides fielded fifteen players. The score at half-time was 0-0 with Villa running out 1-0 victors, courtesy of a goal scored by Jack Hughes. The Aston Villa team that day was: W. Scattergood, W. Weiss, W.H. Price, F. Knight, E. Lee, G. Matthews, H. Matthews, C. Midgley, J. Hughes, W. Such, H. Whateley, G. Page, A. Robbins, W.B. Mason and W. Somers. Apparently the football had been hired for the occasion for a fee of 1s 6d; about 7.5p today.

In 1876 Villa began to play on a new pitch at the Aston Lower Grounds Leisure Park, which was situated opposite the eventual site of Villa Park. The leisure park, opened by a Mr Quilter, offered a wide variety of attractions including wild animals, facilities for tobogganing and rifle-shooting. There was also an aquarium, an ornamental lake set in formal gardens, plus a restaurant and a great hall where various extravaganzas were held. On the sporting side a roller-skating rink augmented a sports pitch that featured football and lacrosse among other sports, and was encircled by a racetrack mainly used for athletics and cycle racing. Incidentally, this was where the legendary Buffalo Bill staged his Wild West Rodeo Show in 1887. Villa didn't stay there long, relocating in 1876 to a rough pitch rented from a local butcher on Wellington Road, Perry Barr. And there they stayed officially until 1897, although the decision to move back to the Lower Grounds had been made in January 1896. The club formed a limited company, the object of which was to raise sufficient capital to develop a ground of their own at Aston Lower Grounds, which at that time was owned by Stratford brewers Flowers. At first the club rented a pitch, again a pretty rough surface, and played the first match there on 17 April 1897.

Many great characters have been associated with Aston Villa over the years, but the names of three Scotsmen stand out in the early years of the club. It was in August 1876 that an enthusiastic Scotsman and brilliant footballer by the name of George Ramsey joined Aston Villa as a player, subsequently being elected to the role of captain. This was the man who masterminded the club's phenomenal rise from its humble beginnings into one of the top teams in the country. In June 1882 injury forced George Ramsey to retire from playing. However, he remained at Villa, and in 1884 became club secretary (manager in today's parlance), responsible for running the team and the club's administrative matters.

Under Ramsey's expert guidance, Aston Villa were victorious on six occasions in the FA Cup, and won the league championship six times, including the Double in 1896/97. He remained club secretary until 1926, later being appointed honorary advisor and subsequently vice-president. A giant in the world of football, George Ramsey died in 1935.

Two years after Ramsay had joined the club, another formidable footballing Scotsman came to Aston Villa, by way of Third Lanark and Ayr Thistle. 'The Old Warhorse', Archie Hunter, contributed his own brand of individual skill to help the club achieve its first taste of FA Cup glory in 1886/87. He was forced out of the game following a heart attack suffered during the match against Everton on 4 January 1890, and sadly he died four years later at the young age of thirty-five.

Already at the club was another Scot, Aston draper William McGregor, who had moved south to Birmingham in 1870. A keen follower of football, McGregor became involved with Aston Villa on the organisational and administrative side. In later years, he became known as the founder of the Football League, for it was he who proposed the idea of formalising the home and away structure for the leading ten or twelve clubs in the country, having learned that a few football clubs in the north of England were considering forming a league. Some months and many discussions later, McGregor called a meeting to discuss his proposals at London's Anderson's Hotel. Eight clubs were represented: Aston Villa, plus Blackburn Rovers, Burnley, Derby County, Notts County, Stoke, West Bromwich Albion and Wolverhampton Wanderers. Strangely, no clubs from the south of the country attended. Progress was made and followed up at a second meeting, this time at the Royal Hotel in Manchester. This time fifteen clubs were represented; the eight from the previous meeting, augmented by Accrington, Bolton Wanderers, Everton, Halliwell (from Sheffield), Nottingham Forest, Preston North End and The Wednesday. Eventually Halliwell, Nottingham Forest and The Wednesday were excluded because of fixture difficulties. Thus, on 2 March 1888, fourteen years after Aston Villa Football Club was formed, the Football League was born. Villa were one of the original twelve members of the Football League, along with Accrington, Blackburn Rovers, Bolton Wanderers, Burnley, Derby County, Everton, Notts County, Preston North End, Stoke City, West Bromwich Albion and Wolverhampton Wanderers.

William McGregor served Aston Villa as vice-president, director, vice-chairman and chairman. He also became chairman of the Football League and the Football Association, and later president of the Football League, being made a life member of the Football League in 1895. This great visionary died in 1911.

Villa's first ever league fixture was away to their Midlands rivals Wolverhampton Wanderers, and was played on Wolves' sloping pitch at Dudley Road, Wolverhampton on 8 September 1888. The Aston Villa team for that first league game was: Warner, Cox, Coulton, Yates, Devey, Dawson, Brown, Green, Allen, Garvey, Hodgetts. Wolves' team was: Baynton, Mason, Baugh, Fletcher, Allen, Lowder, Hunter, Cooper, Anderson, Cannon, White. The game ended in a 1-1 draw. Inside right Tom Green scored for Villa, with an own goal by Villa full-back Gersom Cox for Wolves.

Villa's foundations had been established, but still something was missing. The club needed a more prestigious home to match their footballing aspirations. Before the club had won the League and FA Cup Double in 1896/97, the Aston Villa committee members had decided to accept the offer to move to what was to become their permanent and spiritual home, Villa Park, and thus the legend had begun. Prior to this, Villa had played their home games on a number of different sites, starting off at the Aston Grounds in 1875; Wilson Road, Birchfields from 1875 to 1876; Aston Lower Grounds Meadow from 1875 to 1878 and Wellington Road, Perry Barr from September 1876 to April 1897. However, the quality of some of those pitches left a lot to be desired. Now Villa had a much better playing surface on which to entertain the best teams in the league.

One week prior to Villa's first game at their new ground, on 10 April 1897, they had beaten Everton 3-2 to win the FA Cup for the third time and, in doing so, achieved the Double – league and cup in the same season, equalling the feat of Preston North End in the league's inaugural season. This was the first of two occasions when Villa won back-to-back league championships.

Aston Villa's first game at Villa Park was the 3-0 league victory over Blackburn Rovers on 17 April 1897. Two days later, the second and final home league game of the season saw Villa cruise to a 5-0 win over Wolves. Their spiritual home discovered, Aston Villa went on to experience the extreme

The Villa News and Record, 30 October 1937.

highs, plus a few lows, of life in football's top flight at their Villa Park ground. Aside from their seven championships, seven FA Cups and three League Cups, Aston Villa are also the only West Midlands club to have won the premier European competition – the European Cup, which of course they won in 1981/82.

To all fans of Aston Villa
Happy reading

John Shipley

Season 1980/81

The year 1980 was packed with controversy. High inflation, rising unemployment (now over 2.4 million), deepening recession and the three-day week were among the more prominent events. On the football front, 1980 saw that season's Home International Championship abandoned. The worsening violence of so-called fans, coupled with declining attendances, were problems that needed to be addressed urgently.

One time Villa manager Tommy Docherty once joked that '8,000 supporters would turn up at Villa Park just to watch the kit drying on the line'. Many were of the opinion that those days were clearly over. On 11 August 1980, the Secretaries, Coaches and Managers Association, worried about the direction their sport was taking, published *Soccer – The Fight for Survival*. The study group comprised Alan Dicks, Ken Friar, Harry Haslam, Bill Nicholson, Ron Saunders, Graham Taylor and Terry Venables. The proposals were almost dismissed completely out of hand by the league chairmen at an extraordinary general meeting of the Football League on 9 February 1981. However, they did adopt some of the suggestions, the most prominent being the agreement to introduce three points for a win from the start of season 1981/82.

Aston Villa's form prior to season 1980/81 gave no real indication of their arrival as main contenders for English football's top honour. Their highest league position in recent times had come five years earlier in 1976/77 when they finished fourth in the First Division. Having suffered the ignominy of being relegated to the Second Division in 1966/67, Villa followed this up with relegation to the Third Division in 1969/70, eventually winning promotion back to the Second Division as champions in 1971/72. In total it took Villa eight seasons to regain their position among the nation's elite. New manager Ron Saunders did the trick at his first attempt. Back in the First Division, 1975/76 saw them struggle, finally managing sixteenth in the table. The following season's creditable fourth spot was followed by eighth-place finishes in 1977/78 and 1978/79, and seventh in 1979/80. Progress? Yes – but nothing to indicate what was to follow.

In May 1980, Ron Saunders added striker Peter Withe to the squad. The much-travelled striker chose Villa over a number of clubs, and it was just as well he did because there was bad news on the way. Villa's star striker Brian Little would now not be ready for the start of the new season. His summer cartilage operation had initially gone well, but his recovery hadn't progressed as was hoped. It was a bitter pill for the Villa faithful to have to swallow.

Aston Villa were due to kick-off their 1980/81 championship-winning season at Elland Road, Leeds. The news was that Villa manager Ron Saunders had decided to pin his faith on the team that beat the West German team from Vfl Bochum in the pre-season friendly. Villa's only doubt was Colin Gibson, who had limped off towards the end of the Bochum game with a groin strain. Saunders announced that the full-back would have a late fitness test before the kick-off, and that as cover he had added Eamonn Deacy, the twenty-one-year-old Irish full-back from Galway, who deputised twice when Gibson was injured in the previous season.

LEEDS UNITED *v.* ASTON VILLA

Football League First Division, Elland Road   **Date:** Saturday 16 August 1980
Referee: Mr G.E. Flint (Kirby in Ashfield)   **Attendance:** 23,401

Gary Williams had recovered from his badly bruised ankle to partner Ken McNaught in the centre of Villa's defence in place of the suspended Allan Evans. Colin Gibson failed a late fitness test on a groin strain, so Eamonn Deacy came in at left-back for only his third first-team appearance. He had made his debut in the previous season, ironically at Elland Road. Youngster Gary Shaw would fill in alongside summer signing Peter Withe, following David Geddis' two-match suspension. Leeds manager Jimmy Adamson included Argentinean Alex Sabella, their £400,000 capture from Sheffield United, for his league debut. But the biggest surprise to the Leeds fans was the inclusion of Welshman Carl Harris, who had demanded a transfer earlier in the week.

Villa were shocked inside two minutes of the kick-off when the inexperienced Deacy's flying tackle sent Welshman Brian Flynn sprawling in the penalty area. The penalty followed some nice interplay by Leeds' quartet of Welsh players. Alan Curtis shielded a neat through ball and cleverly found Flynn, who was crudely brought down by the young Irishman. Referee Flint immediately pointed to the penalty spot, and Byron Stevenson confidently sent Rimmer the wrong way to score Leeds' first goal of the season.

Villa hadn't quite recovered their composure when Leeds almost went two up. Carl Harris raced past Deacy and swung the ball to the far post, where Arthur Graham powered in a free header that Jimmy Rimmer saved with his legs. In the eighth minute, Rimmer again rescued Villa when he palmed away Harris's first-time shot from the edge of the area, following some clever interplay with Brian Flynn. Villa's first goal threat came from a hasty Leeds clearance that flew to Tony Morley. However, the winger struck a wild volley well wide of the target. Alex Sabella was making some impressive passes in Leeds' midfield. The Argentinean, who liked to play with his socks rolled down, showed his South American credentials in the twentieth minute when he curled in a corner that arced its way towards the Villa goal. Fortunately, Gary Williams was well positioned and was able to head the ball away.

In the summer Peter Withe had chosen to join Aston Villa in preference to Leeds United, who had also tried to sign him and, naturally, his every move was accompanied by a chorus of boos and catcalls from the home supporters. When he dished out a couple of crunching tackles, one of which left Trevor Cherry writhing in pain, the crowd bayed for his blood!

Two minutes past the half-hour mark, Villa had a great chance to equalise. Withe again showed his strength, after collecting Gordon Cowans' perfect pass, to brush aside Paul Hart's challenge and reached the byline, before whipping in a low centre, which Gary Shaw missed by inches. Leeds came back with an attack down the left. Swain's half-clearance fell to Des Bremner, who unhappily presented Stevenson with the chance to get in a shot but, thankfully, the Leeds man thundered his shot, from fifteen yards, into the side netting.

Leeds United 1	Aston Villa 2
Stevenson (2)	Morley (44)
	Shaw (59)

14

Tony Morley, scorer of Villa's first League goal of the season.

Paul Hart and Trevor Cherry seemed to have learned a quick lesson in keeping a tighter grip on Peter Withe but, in the thirty-seventh minute, the big striker reminded them of his power when he turned brilliantly to whip in a cannonball of a left-foot shot that unfortunately bounced clear off Hart. One minute later, Withe took Des Bremner's shrewd pass in his stride, wrong-footed Stevenson, but saw his shot from a tight angle fisted over the bar by Leeds' 'keeper John Lukic. Seconds before the break, Leeds' players and fans alike were stunned when, from out of nowhere, Villa grabbed an equaliser. The ball came out to Gordon Cowans who looked up, spotted Tony Morley in space twenty yards from goal and clipped a perfect pass to the winger, who turned on a tanner to smash the ball past Lukic inside his near post. Half-time: 1-1.

In the second half Villa came out with all guns blazing, urged on by Dennis Mortimer, ably supported by his midfield cohorts Bremner and Cowans. Leeds were now a shadow of the team that started the game with such a bang, and a period of Villa pressure eventually led to them taking the lead. Lukic's miskicked goal-kick reached Morley, who sped off down the wing before whipping in a great cross to Shaw. The striker flashed in a snap-shot that seemed to hit Brian Greenhoff's arm, before bouncing behind. The players looked at referee Flint just in case he had given a penalty, but no, all he gave was a corner. Then, on fifty-nine minutes, Kenny Swain found Cowans with a free-kick. The midfielder sidestepped a tackle or two before sliding the ball to the unmarked Gary Shaw. With the goal seemingly at his mercy, the young striker cracked in a goal-bound effort that unbelievably Lukic plucked out of the air. It was a marvellous save, but within a minute Villa had scored. Morley evaded two desperate lunging tackles before finding Mortimer, who centred to Peter

15

LEEDS UNITED v. ASTON VILLA

Withe. The Villa number nine missed his kick, but the ball ran to the far post where Gary Shaw swept it beyond Lukic's outstretched arm into the empty net.

The thrills and spills petered out as the game wore on, with Leeds putting on a dismal show in total contrast to their self-assured performance in the first period. Villa were more than content to take all the points in a 2-1 victory. After the game Ron Saunders said he thought his team showed a lot of character for coming back with such determination and spirit.

FA Disciplinary Committee boss Bert Millichip warned all footballers to cut out the professional foul or face the consequences. Scary stuff! The Baggies' chairman felt that Arsenal's Willie Young should have been sent off for indiscriminately chopping down West Ham's seventeen-year-old Paul Allen in the previous season's FA Cup final. All West Ham got was a free-kick outside the box. In Bert's opinion, players didn't care about being shown a yellow card 'and the sooner referees start sending the players off, the better, and that is the committee's intention this season'. FA records show that the previous season 114 players were sent off in the league, FA Cup and League Cup; three fewer than 1978/79, but eight more than 1977/78.

Two points at Leeds United was a great start. Could Villa choke the Canaries from East Anglia?

Leeds United: Lukic, Cherry, Stevenson, Flynn, Hart, Greenhoff B., Gray E., Harris, Curtis, Sabella, Graham A.
   Sub: Parlane.

Aston Villa: Rimmer, Swain, Deacy, Williams, McNaught, Mortimer, Bremner, Shaw, Withe, Cowans, Morley.
   Sub: Ormsby.

ASTON VILLA v. NORWICH CITY

Football League First Division, Villa Park

Referee: Mr S. Bates (Bristol)

Date: Wednesday 20 August 1980

Attendance: 25,970

This was a disappointingly low Villa Park turn out after the excellent away win at Elland Road. It had been expected that a lot more than 26,000 would come to watch Villa's first home game of the season. Ron Saunders later pointed out that, from his experience, Norwich have never brought many supporters to the Midlands. He also stressed other factors, such as the recession and the holiday season, and pointed to the fact that the previous night's visit of champions Liverpool to Coventry had only attracted a gate of 22,807 people. Twenty-one-year-old Gordon Cowans' performance against Leeds brought widespread calls for England boss Ron Greenwood to include him in the full England team for the opening game of England's World Cup campaign against Norway on 10 September. As we now know, he didn't! In fact it wasn't until 23 February 1983 that Cowans finally won his first of 10 caps.

Ron Saunders was pleased to have Allan Evans back and Colin Gibson returned at left-back, with Deacy dropping down to the substitutes' bench. Norwich manager John Bond named an unchanged side from the one that had walloped Stoke City 5-1 at home on Saturday.

Defensively minded Norwich came for a draw, clearly hoping to take home a point by frustrating Villa with their negative tactics. The Canaries packed all ten outfield players behind the ball whenever Villa had possession. The crowd too were getting irritated as all too often they watched Villa's attacks run out of steam against a solid wall of no-nonsense defenders. Norwich simply refused to attack, despite having Joe Royle and Justin Fashanu in their team. Attack after attack foundered on the seemingly impenetrable Norwich wall in which twin destroyers-in-chief, Kevin Bond and Tony Powell, gave a marvellous display of defensive ability in an often-crowded penalty area.

Skipper Dennis Mortimer continued to force his men forward and once more led the way in the twenty-first minute when a powerful run through the middle ended with a disappointing shot that sailed over the crossbar. Immediately, Peter Withe picked out Gordon Cowans with a deft touch, but somehow the Villa midfielder wasted Villa's best chance of the match by dragging his shot wide. Undeterred, Cowans kept up his tremendous work rate, at the same time demonstrating just why Bobby Robson and other league managers rated him so highly, spraying immaculate pass after immaculate pass around the park. Surely Villa would get a breakthrough soon. The way Norwich were playing it was difficult to see how they had scored five goals against Stoke. Youngster Gary Shaw had a couple of half chances that he didn't make the most of, giving the impression that the Villa players had left their shooting boots at home, as each attempt on goal either finished wide or was boomed over the bar. Thankfully the referee blew his whistle to bring to a close a dour and disappointing first half that must have tested even the staunchest of supporters' patience. The teams left the field to a chorus of jeering from large sections of the crowd. Half-time: 0-0.

Aston Villa 1   Norwich City 0
Shaw (76)

ASTON VILLA v. NORWICH CITY

Allan Evans holds off Norwich's Justin Fashanu and Kevin Bond.

It was more of the same at the start of the second half. Cowans continued to show that he was head and shoulders above every other player on the park. He delivered each pass with outstanding technical finesse. There were clever flicks and strong running; all good stuff, but each time there was either Bond or Powell to get the ball away. Eventually Villa gave their fans something to cheer when Gary Shaw's persistence was rewarded with a goal.

The goal came after seventy-six minutes, following a slight lapse of concentration on the part of the Norwich defenders. Tony Morley found Peter Withe, who flicked the ball into the path of Shaw. The young striker took deliberate aim from twenty yards and whipped in a tremendous shot that flew past Norwich 'keeper Roger Hansbury to huge cheers and sighs of relief, ending three-quarters-of-an-hour of sheer frustration for Villa and their fans. This was Shaw's fourth real scoring chance, which made one wonder why he hadn't taken any of the other three; on another day he would at least have notched a hat-trick.

Shaw's goal suddenly spurred Norwich into attacking mode; they had lost the point they came for so now there was nothing to lose in going for the equaliser. As the Canaries came forward they began to leave gaps in midfield and at the back, which led to a much more open final ten minutes, during which Norwich swung over some dangerous-looking crosses. But Villa fans needn't have worried because Ken McNaught and Allan Evans marshalled Joe Royle superbly and neither he nor Justin Fashanu managed to get in a telling effort on the Villa goal. Villa pressed forward into the spaces yielded by Norwich looking for a second goal and were a tad unlucky not to score. First Gary Shaw was only an inch or so off target with a shot on the turn after Des Bremner had put him through, and then the blond striker ran onto a defence-splitting pass from Allan Evans, only to see his goal-bound shot bounce off a defender for a corner. Back came Shaw for another go and this time Roger Hansbury leapt magnificently to turn his elegant lob over the bar.

In the dying minutes a fabulous header from Peter Withe beat the Norwich goalkeeper, but was cleared off the line by Greg Downs, and in the end Villa ran out worthy winners of a frustrating game, which included many encouraging performances by key players, particularly Cowans who, despite suffering from a chest and throat virus, which restricted his influence on this game, again demonstrated his burgeoning ability to become one of the all-time great Villa playmakers.

With the first two league games played Villa were up at the top with Ipswich, Sunderland and Tottenham, who all had four points. Now for a trip up north to meet Manchester City at Maine Road.

Aston Villa: Rimmer, Swain, Gibson, Evans, McNaught, Mortimer, Bremner, Shaw, Withe, Cowans, Morley. Sub: Deacy.

Norwich City: Hansbury, McDowell, Downs, Mendham, Bond, Powell, Woods, Fashanu, Royle, Paddon, Goble (Nightingale).

MANCHESTER CITY v. ASTON VILLA

Football League First Division, Maine Road   **Date:** Saturday 23 August 1980
Referee: Mr I. Saunders (Newcastle-upon-Tyne)   **Attendance:** 30,017

Villa's only change was on the substitutes' bench, where Gary Williams was named ahead of Deacy. City, who had lost both their opening games, made a number of changes. Villa fans' expectancy was high as City hadn't yet scored a goal but had conceded seven.

The game started quietly with neither side creating too much of a threat to the other's goal. Then, in the ninth minute, Peter Withe back-heeled the ball to Gary Shaw. The youngster charged through the City defence before returning the ball perfectly to Withe, who in one movement chested the ball down and cracked an unstoppable volley past big Joe Corrigan in the City goal. Moments later the referee leniently delivered a lecture to City defender Tommy Booth after he had blatantly handled Tony Morley's cross to prevent it reaching Peter Withe. It was clearly a bookable offence. Villa failed to capitalise on the resultant free-kick when Allan Evans was adjudged to be offside by the linesman. Villa continued to press the City defence with some lovely football, prompted by the superb passing of Cowans, which at times had City at sixes and sevens. However, Villa were a little fortunate when Kevin Reeves laid the ball into the path of Steve MacKenzie for the midfielder to crack in a first-time thunderbolt that screamed wide of Rimmer's goal. Back came Villa with Gordon Cowans again showing his class, delivering a stunning forty-yard crossfield pass to Morley who, in turn, fed the ball through to Peter Withe, but before the Villa striker could get in a shot, Joe Corrigan sprinted out to boot the ball away.

In the twenty-third minute City mounted a sweeping attack that almost brought a goal. Paul Sugrue sent Paul Power away down the right wing before thumping in a shot from a tight angle that whizzed past the out-rushing Jimmy Rimmer into the side netting. Minutes later, Peter Withe took the ball to the edge of the City penalty area before powering in a stinging left-foot drive, which brought an athletic diving save from 'keeper Corrigan who palmed the ball behind for a corner. On thirty-seven minutes, Colin Gibson swung over a free-kick from the left. Peter Withe rose above the City defenders, but his free header lacked any real power and Corrigan comfortably plucked the ball out of the air. On forty-three minutes, Peter Withe got on the end of another cracking move with a burst of acceleration into the City box, but sadly Gary Shaw hadn't kept up with play to meet the centre forward's chip into the middle. Mortimer was racing in at the far post, but was unable to reach the ball. Half-time: City 0 Villa 1.

Whatever City manager Malcolm Allison said during the break worked wonders, because his players underwent a metamorphosis into a proper football team. They began the second half with a Dennis Tueart raid that Ken McNaught scrambled clear. Then Nicky Reid burst through, but failed to trouble Rimmer with a tame low shot. Suddenly City looked more dangerous. However, their main strike force was being well shackled by McNaught and Evans. Villa came back with a dazzling run

Manchester City 2	Aston Villa 2
Tueart (83)	Withe 2 (9 & 76)
Ranson (88)	

Manchester City v. Aston Villa

Villa's two-goal hero
Peter Withe.

by Gary Shaw that saw him torture the City defence, before Withe's twenty-five-yard piledriver was brilliantly saved by Corrigan, who dived low to smother the ball. Seconds later, Withe returned the complement with a shrewd pass to Shaw. The young striker's enthusiastic brio took him a few strides further before he attempted an audacious curler that Corrigan did well to reach. Tony Morley had come in for quite a bit of harsh treatment from Nicky Reid and, finally, in the fifty-ninth minute the referee had had enough and booked the City man for chopping the winger down. Morley needed treatment from the old wet sponge before he was able to resume.

Jimmy Rimmer's end of the pitch had been quiet for a while, but in the sixty-seventh minute the Villa 'keeper had to show his pedigree with an incredible save to prevent City from scoring. Reid made ground down the right flank and swung over a nasty looking cross to the unmarked Dennis Tueart, who powered in a header from close range that looked destined for the net, but somehow Rimmer managed to fling his body across his goal to push the ball over the bar. Paul Sugrue had been limping for some time, and was substituted by Roger Palmer. The corner came to nothing and Villa swept back into the attack. Then, in the seventy-sixth minute, they got the second goal that should have put the seal on a fine victory. Peter Withe's second goal came from another great leap above the City defenders, his powerful header zipping past Corrigan's outstretched hand.

Manchester City v. Aston Villa

With only seven minutes left to play Villa were cruising to a third win on the trot. Then disaster struck. An innocuous centre was floated into the Villa box. The players jumped, and the referee blew his whistle. Villa's defenders couldn't believe their eyes when Mr Saunders, the referee not Ron, pointed to the spot. Yes, he had awarded a penalty, apparently for handball. The Villa players swarmed round the official, protesting vehemently, but to no avail. After the kerfuffle had died down, Dennis Tueart stepped up to the plate and tucked a low shot past Rimmer. Okay, it was bad luck, and these things happen, but with less than two minutes remaining, Lady Luck decided to pull the plug completely. City full-back Ray Ranson sent in a speculative low shot that Rimmer appeared to have covered, until the ball took a cruel deflection to scrape inside the near post. It was a bitter pill to swallow, and there was hardly any time left to do much about it.

Villa had to trudge back to Birmingham with only one point instead of two – a travesty of justice. Thankfully, Ipswich and Tottenham also drew and Sunderland lost, but Southampton won again, so now four teams had 5 points.

Manchester City: Corrigan, Ranson, Reid, Booth, Caton, MacKenzie, Tueart, Daly, Sugrue (Palmer), Power, Reeves.

Aston Villa: Rimmer, Swain, Gibson, Evans, McNaught, Mortimer, Bremner, Shaw, Withe, Cowans, Morley. Sub: Williams.

Aston Villa v. Leeds United

League Cup Second Round First Leg, Villa Park   **Date:** Wednesday 27 August 1980
Referee: Mr C. White (Middlesex)   **Attendance:** 23,622

Unchanged Villa had Deacy back on the bench for the first leg of this League Cup tie at Villa Park. Leeds made a number of changes to the team that faced Villa in the opening game of the season. In came England defender Paul Madeley, Brian Greenhoff switching to left-back, and of their Welsh contingent only Brian Flynn had the opportunity to test Villa again. In fact Villa completely dominated this cup tie, but worryingly botched most of their chances to score. As far as entertainment value went, Villa were always good value and should really have scored a hatful of goals rather than just the one they got. Villa just about shaded the early exchanges without creating much in the way of clear chances, but all that changed in the ninth minute. Peter Withe began the move in the middle of the field, his accurate pass finding Des Bremner, who made a little ground before Colin Gibson took over, surging down the left and threading the ball to Villa's talismanic captain Dennis Mortimer, who went racing down the wing to send in a peach of a cross. Tony Morley met the ball perfectly at the far post with a scorching left-foot volley that Leeds' goalkeeper John Lukic managed to get his hands to, but could only divert the ball into the corner of his own net. Now Villa were completely bossing the game, but chance after chance was frittered away by over-anxious shooting or trying to walk the ball in. However, Villa should have gone two up when Gary Shaw burst through the visitors' defence and into the box, only to be pushed over from behind. It was a clear-cut penalty, but referee White turned away Villa's loud appeals and waved play on.

Leeds' central-defensive pivot Paul Madeley was being given a hard time by Peter Withe. However, the England man combined well with Brian Greenhoff to thwart Gary Shaw after he and Gordon Cowans had produced a move of exquisite speed and skill, turning the defenders inside out, before Madeley managed to scramble the ball away. Cowans was in excellent form, working tirelessly alongside his fellow midfielders. His balance and composure and deftness of passing delighted the fans with each beguiling touch. On the right, Des Bremner covered the ground in front of Kenny Swain, always prepared to out-fight his opponents for possession of the ball, as was his skipper, who produced a series of his trademark lung-bursting runs from deep. These three driving midfielders gave Villa an altogether different dimension to that of Leeds.

Just prior to the half-hour the referee surprised players and crowd alike by booking Allan Evans for what appeared to be a fair tackle on Alex Sabella. The Argentinean hit the ground like he had been poleaxed, and followed this up with a bit of synchronised writhing, and maybe that influenced the black-clad official; either way it seemed a bit harsh especially after he had allowed the Leeds defenders leniency in similar situations. Not long after it looked odds-on a second goal for Villa when Gary Shaw ran onto a tremendous through ball to fire in a blistering shot that rebounded to safety off John Lukic's legs. Somehow Leeds had managed to weather the storm, but with the clock

Aston Villa 1   Leeds United 0
    Morley (9)

Aston Villa v. Leeds United

Aston Villa manager Ron Saunders.

ticking down to the interval, Tony Morley boldly accelerated away from his marker once again to force his way into the area, but sadly spurned the opportunity to score by dragging a ferocious shot into the side netting with only Lukic to beat. Half-time: Villa 1 Leeds 0.

After the break, Villa continued where they had left off and a series of half-chances went begging; the Leeds defence was certainly riding its luck. But still Villa couldn't find the means to that elusive second goal. So far Leeds hadn't looked too interested in getting the ball forward with any real conviction. They seemed content to let Villa come at them with all guns blazing, confident in their ability to hang onto a one-goal deficit. Withe and Shaw went close a couple of times and then, as the game moved into its final stages, the visitors sensed that there might be a chance of an equaliser. Centre forward Terry Connor cracked in a shot that went agonisingly close, before the same player tested Jimmy Rimmer with a speculative effort. Apart from these, plus a couple of long-range efforts, Villa's defence retained an air of confidence. On another day Villa's hungry forwards might have scored four or five. To some extent, the game was spoiled by a number of refereeing decisions that smacked of inconsistency. Some of the rulings were baffling, particularly the denial of Gary Shaw's obvious penalty claim, and in view of Mr White's subsequent leniency, his decision to book Allan Evans was ridiculous.

Ron Saunders was delighted with the win and the performance of his players, but disappointed that his team hadn't converted their domination into more goals. For Leeds, goalkeeper John Lukic had been in tremendous form, plus he had had that little bit of luck to keep his side in the two-legged tie. Villa would have their work cut out to finish the job in the second leg at Elland Road in a week's time.

Villa transfer-listed six players, including former Scottish international Alex Cropley who, despite going on loan to Newcastle United the previous season, had failed to regain a regular place after breaking his leg in 1977. Also listed were Gary Shelton, Ivor Linton, Willie Young, Lee Jenkins and Duncan Heath.

Aston Villa: Rimmer, Swain, Gibson, Evans, McNaught, Mortimer, Bremner, Shaw, Withe, Cowans, Morley.
  Sub: Deacy.
Leeds United: Lukic, Cherry, Greenhoff, Flynn, Hart, Madeley, Chandler, Thomas, Connor, Sabella, Graham.
  Sub: Gray.

ASTON VILLA v. COVENTRY CITY

Football League First Division, Villa Park
Referee: Mr A. Porter (Bolton)

Date: Saturday 30 August 1980
Attendance: 26,050

Ron Saunders named an unchanged side, with Pat Heard at substitute in place of Deacy. The Sky Blues were forced into a number of changes from the side that had beaten Manchester United 1-0 at Old Trafford in the League Cup. Their decidedly young-looking team included nineteen-year-old debutant Clive Haywood in place of axed Belgian international Roger van Gool, and young Mark Hateley, in for injured centre forward Garry Thompson, only four hours after arriving back from a spell in American soccer.

The first five minutes of the game were packed with incident. First we had a disallowed goal. Tony Morley whizzed down the wing, played a clever one-two with Peter Withe and ended with a tremendous shot that almost broke the net. The referee's whistle brought to an end a brief moment of joy as the winger was judged to have been in an offside position when the ball came back to him. Just after central defender Gary Gillespie was hurt and had to be substituted by eighteen-year-old Danny Thomas. Then Coventry midfielder Andy Blair tried a long-range grubber that squirmed just wide of Rimmer's post. Villa hit back, and goalkeeper Jim Blyth had Sky Blue hearts in mouths when, attempting to clear a dangerous through ball, he completely missed his kick. The ball smacked into Peter Withe and ran to Gary Shaw, who whipped it back into the middle. However, the Coventry 'keeper managed to fist the ball away before Withe could get his head to it. It was thrilling end-to-end stuff, with neither side able to stamp their authority on the game.

It was Villa's turn again. Withe chased a hopeful long through ball into the visitors' penalty area, but Paul Dyson got there first to put the ball behind for a corner, which came to nothing. Then it was Coventry, mounting an attack down the right wing that Colin Gibson seemed to have covered, but the referee adjudged that he had fouled Haywood in the process. Blair's free-kick was clipped to the near post where, fortunately, Tommy English glanced his header over the crossbar. Villa were certainly under the cosh, this time from another needless free-kick on the right. Thomas floated a high ball into the box and Rimmer started to come out but, realising that he wouldn't make it, back-pedalled towards his line and was stranded as Hateley skimmed the bar with a powerful header.

On twenty-eight minutes Gordon Cowans attempted a half-hearted back-pass to Jimmy Rimmer without looking. The ball ran to Tommy English, who was lurking in the way of the intended target, but Villa were let off the hook when the ball skimmed off the striker's foot for a goal-kick. The visitors kept up the pressure and might have gone ahead five minutes later when Hateley centred towards the far post from the left, but Gerry Daly hurried his shot and Rimmer was able to get in a block at the foot of his post.

At last Villa managed to break out from Coventry's attacking spree to force a left-wing corner. Gordon Cowans whipped over an in-swinger and Allan Evans out-jumped the defenders to send

Aston Villa 1	Coventry City 0
Shaw (65)	

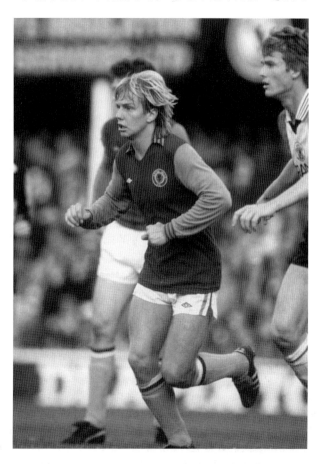

Gary Shaw.

in a header. Unfortunately, ex-Villa player Steve Hunt was perfectly positioned on the goal-line to head the ball clear. As the first half neared the end, the heavens opened. Tony Morley centred from the right, but Des Bremner's diving header missed the ball by a fraction. Then a left-wing cross from Colin Gibson should have produced a goal, but Gary Shaw followed the pattern of the day by putting his header over the top. Half-time: 0-0.

Villa began the second half in a much more aggressive manner and immediately had Coventry's defenders stretched. Attack after attack was repulsed by the Sky Blues, who suddenly didn't look anywhere near as comfortable as they had earlier in the game. Cowans and Mortimer were at the heart of a number of promising attacks, the best of which saw Morley smash in a blistering left-foot volley that Blyth gratefully gathered into his body. The Coventry 'keeper was being kept busy by Villa's forwards and had to get down smartly at his near post to block a stinging cross-shot from Peter Withe. By now the playing surface had become decidedly slippery with many of the players struggling to keep their feet. But it was Villa that coped better with the slippery conditions and in the sixty-fifth minute, their attacking onslaught bought the goal they so longed for. Dennis Mortimer curled in a right-wing corner and, as the ball sped into the crowded goalmouth, Gary Shaw reached it first to glance a fine header just inside the far post.

ASTON VILLA v. COVENTRY CITY

Coventry's reshuffled defence had done pretty well for just over an hour but, following Villa's goal they were constantly pushed back into their own half, at times defending desperately. Villa skipper Dennis Mortimer was inspirational, prompting almost every attack as his team stepped up their attacking momentum. However, the elusive second goal just would not come.

Sky Blues 'keeper Jim Blyth was magnificent, preventing Villa from notching three or four goals in a second half full of non-stop attacking. In the seventy-fifth minute Villa almost paid the penalty for failing to put their chances away, when a sudden Sky Blues breakaway looked to have brought the equaliser. Ex-Villa man Steve Hunt darted through to crack in a fierce shot that beat Jimmy Rimmer, only to rattle the woodwork and bounce clear. What a let off!

Fortunately, after that scare Villa regained control of the game and forced a couple more saves from Blyth in the final ten minutes. It maintained a great start to the league season for Villa, with three wins and a draw. Third place in the league table on goal difference was marvellous.

Of the other top teams, Tottenham lost 2-0 at Arsenal, Ipswich beat Everton 4-0 and Southampton beat the Blues 3-1, leaving Ipswich and Saints in first and second place respectively.

The top of the First Division table:

	PLD	W	D	L	F	A	PTS
Ipswich Town	4	3	1	0	9	2	7
Southampton	4	3	1	0	8	3	7
Aston Villa	**4**	**3**	**1**	**0**	**6**	**3**	**7**
Sunderland	4	2	1	1	9	4	5
Liverpool	4	2	1	1	7	3	5
Nottm Forest	4	2	1	1	7	3	5

Aston Villa: Rimmer, Swain, Gibson, Evans, McNaught, Mortimer, Bremner, Shaw, Withe, Cowans, Morley.
   Sub: Heard.
Coventry City: Blyth, Coop, Roberts, Blair, Dyson, Gillespie (Thomas), Haywood, Daly, Hateley, English, Hunt S.

LEEDS UNITED *v.* ASTON VILLA

League Cup Second Round Second Leg, Elland Road
Referee: Mr J.D. Hough (Macclesfield)

Date: Wednesday 3 September 1980
Attendance: 12,236

Villa's lethal striking duo Peter Withe and Gary Shaw sank sad Leeds in this second leg game with an almost faultless display to maintain Villa's unbeaten start to the season. The game was only six minutes old when Peter Withe silenced the tiny Elland Road crowd with his third goal of the season to put Villa two ahead on aggregate. Tony Morley made a trademark dash down the wing and whipped over a perfect cross for the Villa number nine to power a stunning header past John Lukic in the Leeds goal.

However, after a poor start to the game Leeds suddenly came alive. The move that brought the equaliser began with some inspirational tackling by their Welsh terrier in midfield, Brian Flynn. He got the ball forward to the powerful Terry Connor who, in turn, surged past Colin Gibson on the right before curling in a dangerous cross that fizzed across Villa's goalmouth. Derek Parlane headed the ball back into the centre where Arthur Graham, with his back to goal, executed a tremendously athletic thirteenth-minute scissor-kick that had Jimmy Rimmer beaten all the way. The goal momentarily stunned Villa, who were now pushed back by a resurgent Leeds.

Leeds, who obviously scented blood, had Villa on the back foot for the rest of the half. Their spirited revival frequently threatened to be rewarded with a second goal that would have brought the aggregate score level. It was a worrying time for Villa's all-too-often spread-eagled defence, but one of great delight to the Leeds supporters. Throughout this period of intense pressure Jimmy Rimmer put in a full shift to deny a series of efforts from the baying Leeds forwards, including one breathtakingly brilliant save to prevent Leeds from getting back into the tie. Then some great defending from Villa's centre-backs Evans and McNaught stopped Leeds from scoring again. And then with just seconds to go to the break, and totally against the run of play, Gary Shaw popped up with a goal to soothe Villa's nerves. Gordon Cowans showed his skilful pedigree, threading his way through the Leeds defence before sliding a perfect pass into Shaw's run. The young striker took instant aim and pulled the trigger with a scorching shot that must have stung Lukic's hands as he parried the ball. The rebound looked as though it would fall to Cowans, but Gary Shaw rushed in to meet it first to lash it into the net. Half-time: Leeds 1 Villa 2.

A second-half fightback from Leeds failed to materialise, and it was Villa that always looked the most likely to grab another goal. Twenty-five minutes of controlled football from Villa took the sting out of Leeds in a typical display of excellent teamwork coupled with some exceptional individual performances that were epitomised by Peter Withe, Gary Shaw and the outstanding Gordon Cowans. This play was rewarded on seventy-two minutes with a third goal for Villa, scored by Gary Shaw.

Apart from Ken McNaught being booked for a foul, everything at Villa Park was looking rosy, but at Leeds the stormclouds over manager Jimmy Adamson were growing. The call for his head was

Leeds United 1	Aston Villa 3
Graham (13)	Withe (6)
	Shaw 2 (45 & 72)

Aston Villa won 3-1 on the night, 4-1 on aggregate.

LEEDS UNITED v. ASTON VILLA

Villa's deadly duo, Gary Shaw and
Peter Withe, pre-season 1982.

vividly demonstrated by the fans' chants that Adamson must go, and with this 4-1 aggregate defeat it seemed that he had lost any chance of survival in his job.

At times Leeds really weren't that bad, but once Villa had weathered the hard-fought first half, which often throbbed with competitiveness and attractive attacking football from both sides, there was only one winner, and that was Aston Villa.

In the news this week, England cricket captain Ian Botham announced that he had abandoned his plan to play football for Scunthorpe United next autumn. Beefy's decision was based on his desire to concentrate on cricket and be fully focused on preparing to lead England in their tour of the West Indies, which started in January 1981.

In the draw for the third round of the League Cup, Aston Villa would have to travel to Cambridge United who had beaten Wolves in the second round. The daunting task of meeting another Midlands team meant that history would repeat itself inside a year, because in last season's FA Cup fourth round Villa had been held to a 1-1 draw at the Abbey Stadium before winning the replay 4-1 at Villa Park. The bookies priced Villa at 8-1 to win the League Cup. Liverpool were favourites at 3-1, holders Forest at 4-1, Ipswich and Arsenal 6-1. Watford's incredible 7-1 comeback to beat Southampton impressed many people, but not the bookmakers. Drawn away to Sheffield Wednesday, Elton John's team were quoted at 125-1.

Villa's next trip was to Suffolk, to face highly fancied Ipswich, managed by Bobby Robson. The good news was that Jimmy Rimmer had won his race to be fit for the game. It was just the sort of boost they needed for the clash with top of the table Ipswich at Portman Road. Jimmy had injured his thigh during the Leeds game, but had come through a late fitness test with flying colours, so Villa would be unchanged.

Leeds United: Lukic, Cherry, Greenhoff, Flynn, Hart, Madeley, Parlane, Hamson (Harris), Connor, Sabella, Graham.

Aston Villa: Rimmer, Swain, Gibson, Evans, McNaught, Mortimer, Bremner, Shaw (Deacy), Withe, Cowans, Morley.

IPSWICH TOWN v. ASTON VILLA

Football League First Division, Portman Road
Referee: Mr M.J. Bidmead (Chessington)

Date: Saturday 6 September 1980
Attendance: 23,192

The wheels came off here, and it was a shame really. Bobby Robson's high-flying Ipswich were unbeaten in four games and at the top of the table. The Suffolk Blues were strong at the back, creative in midfield, with a sharp attack that to date had scored nine goals and conceded only two. Ron Saunders chose Eamonn Deacy over Gary Williams for the substitute's role. Steve McCall came in for Ipswich's England defender Mick Mills, who was forced to miss the game with an ankle injury.

Villa started brim-full of confidence and Gary Shaw won a right-wing corner in the second minute. The ball came out to Mortimer on the edge of the penalty area who cracked in a cannonball of a shot that Paul Cooper fisted clear at full stretch. Then Tony Morley escaped the clutches of George Burley and sped into the box, but rifled his venomous effort into the crowd. Ipswich immediately swept downfield to create a shooting chance for Paul Mariner, but the England striker ballooned the ball high over the bar.

Ipswich were playing some mouth-watering football that had the crowd drooling with anticipation, and in a five-minute spell won four corners that Villa defended stoutly. Ipswich's brand of meticulous build-up play was in stark contrast to Villa's more direct approach; their two Dutchmen Muhren and Thijssen moving the ball around with consummate ease. Muhren got down the left again before forcing Rimmer to grope at his swerving cross, knocking the ball down into his own area, where Allan Evans was able to boot it clear. But Villa were not to be outdone and hit back with a fine shot on the run from Colin Gibson that Cooper clutched gratefully to his chest. Villa swept forward again with lovely interplay between Morley, Withe and Mortimer that ended with a brilliant overhead kick by Gary Shaw that rebounded off John Wark's body. Gordon Cowans nearly caught out Ipswich with an exquisite left-foot chip that beat the home side's attempted offside trap. Gary Shaw had timed his run into the box to perfection to head the ball unselfishly across goal, but the ball was too far ahead of Withe, and the chance went begging. Then Rimmer had to dive smartly to push away a Mariner shot for a corner, followed by Alan Brazil turning Ken McNaught inside-out on the right before whipping in a cross that Muhren fired straight into Rimmer's arms. During this spell, Villa were forced back by the power and intensity of Ipswich's attacks. Gibson lost the ball to Eric Gates on the left to fire over a tantalising cross that Brazil volleyed past the post.

Villa got going again with Cowans tricking his way past a couple of players to slide a pass inside the full-back to Gary Shaw, who slipped the ball to Morley, but the winger's shot-cum-cross skimmed the top of the crossbar. With the seconds ticking away to half-time, Shaw fed the ball back to Withe, only to see the big striker's shot cannon away off a defender's leg. Then Mortimer headed just wide of the post. With the whistle poised at the referee's lips, Villa had a fabulous chance to snatch the

Ipswich Town 1
Thijssen (56)

Aston Villa 0

Ipswich Town v. Aston Villa

David Geddis.

lead. First Swain then Withe failed to react quickly enough, followed by Morley and Shaw in much the same way. All had simple chances to put the ball away, but dwelt far too long and so wasted the chance to put the ball into the net. Half-time: 0-0.

At the start of the second half Gibson brought down Alan Brazil on the edge of the area. Muhren's well-struck free-kick was spectacularly saved by Jimmy Rimmer, but the referee had already blown for offside. Then came a series of dangerous incidents at both ends. On fifty-four minutes Eric Gates thundered in a shot that cannoned off Evans before scraping the bar. At the other end Morley floated over a delightful centre that Gary Shaw met with power, but his header hit Cooper's leg and rebounded to safety. A minute later Ipswich took the lead. Eric Gates darted down the left and sent a short pass to Dutchman Frans Thijssen, who shot first time. Allan Evans managed to half-stop the shot on the line but, sadly for Villa, the ball squirmed into the net.

It was a bitter blow for Villa and heralded a period of even more Ipswich pressure. From back to front Ipswich looked extremely good and so very strong, and gradually stifled Villa's midfield threat. Their two Dutch midfielders, now with the upper hand, pushed further up the pitch to support their attack. Villa weren't going to lie down without a fight and dug deep into their reserves of stamina and willpower, with Mortimer leading a defiant late fightback that might have produced a better finish. Morley fired over when well placed, then good efforts from Bremner, Withe, Shaw and Mortimer brought nothing but corners. But in the end this late flourish wasn't to prove good enough, and Frans Thijssen's goal robbed Villa of their unbeaten record.

Gary Shaw missed a hatful of chances that, with steadier finishing, might have yielded a hat-trick. Withe and Morley could, and probably should, have scored. At times Ron Saunders' men outplayed their Suffolk rivals and, had they taken their chances, they might have wrapped up the game before half-time. Ipswich were now unbeaten in five games, topping the table from Southampton on goal difference. These were the only teams with 9 points.

First Division table after 5 league games:

	PLD	W	D	L	F	A	PTS
Ipswich Town	5	4	1	0	10	2	9
Southampton	5	4	1	0	11	4	9
Sunderland	5	3	1	1	10	4	7
Aston Villa	**5**	**3**	**1**	**1**	**6**	**4**	**7**
Liverpool	5	2	2	1	8	4	6
Nottm Forest	5	2	1	1	7	3	6

The headline grabber this week was the rising hooliganism that infested football. On 6 September, following the sending off of Terry Curran at Oldham, hundreds of Sheffield Wednesday fans ran amok. Amid a hail of bottles and bricks, the game was held up for around half an hour. This nasty incident reportedly reduced Owls' manager Jack Charlton to tears. On the same day after Boro's game with Nottingham Forest, a young Middlesbrough fan had his head smashed in outside Ayresome Park. West Ham were forced to play the second leg of their European Cup Winners' Cup match against Castilla behind closed doors because of the drunken behaviour of a number of their fans during the first leg in the Bernabeu Stadium in Madrid on 17 September.

Ipswich Town: Cooper, Burley, McCall, Thijssen, Osman, Butcher, Wark, Muhren, Mariner, Brazil, Gates.
    Sub: O'Callaghan.
Aston Villa: Rimmer, Swain, Gibson, Evans, McNaught, Mortimer, Bremner, Shaw, Withe, Cowans, Morley.
    Sub: Deacy.

ASTON VILLA v. EVERTON

Football League First Division, Villa Park
Referee: Mr B.H. Daniels (Brentwood)

Date: Saturday 13 September 1980
Attendance: 25,673

Unlucky for some, this thirteenth was not a good day for Villa. Their performance wasn't anywhere near what was needed from a team with title aspirations. Villa's creativity simply dried up as they allowed Everton to claim their first away win in twenty-five games. One of the most alarming aspects of this game was Villa's failure to test the Everton goalkeeper Jim McDonagh. It was a bitterly disappointing afternoon for the fans.

Unchanged Villa had Gary Williams on the substitute's bench in place of Eamonn Deacy. Former Villa favourite John Gidman was at right-back for the visitors.

Everton sprinted out of the blocks to give Villa a headache in the first minute when Joe McBride chased a through ball and Jimmy Rimmer had to race off his line to boot the ball clear. Villa countered with a break down the right, but the move was halted when Mortimer's chipped pass caught Morley fractionally offside. Villa weren't convincing and, when Everton hit back, an untidy piece of play between Cowans and Swain was almost punished, but fortunately Des Bremner was able to reach the ball first to clear the danger. For several long minutes, both teams seemed content to play it safe by hitting long back-passes to their goalkeepers. On ten minutes, Des Bremner chanced his arm with a twenty-five-yarder that deflected behind for a corner. Dennis Mortimer's flag-kick nearly produced a goal, but Bremner's looping header was booted off the line by John Bailey. Gidman was booed every time he touched the ball, until his twenty-five-yard back-pass passed well wide of his 'keeper. When the ball looked to be heading for the Everton net, the jeers turned to cheers, but when the ball drifted the wrong side of the post, the booing returned. Then Allan Evans tried a first-time dipping half-volley from Mortimer's right-wing free-kick, but the ball flew narrowly wide.

Midway through the half, Everton hit Villa with a lightening counterattack. Asa Hartford combined well with Bob Latchford to tee up an opportunity for Peter Eastoe, but the former Wolves striker's first-time volley screamed well over the top. When Gordon Cowans fouled Steve McMahon just after the half-hour, Rimmer had to scramble across his goal to push Gidman's swinging free-kick behind for what was to prove to be a very costly corner. When the flag-kick flew into the box Mike Lyons rose above everyone to thump a powerful header past Rimmer.

Four minutes later, Everton went further ahead. Joe McBride tricked his way past Kenny Swain on the left and whipped in a curling cross that was met perfectly by the inrushing Eastoe, whose brave header flew past the helpless Rimmer. Eastoe needed treatment to a head wound and, when he resumed, his shirt was stained with blood.

Two Everton goals in four minutes clearly rocked Villa, who suddenly came to life, trying to move the ball around more urgently. Everton countered by packing their defence so tightly that Villa struggled to mount any kind of cohesive attack and create even the smallest of chances. With Villa's defence and midfield pushing forward to support the attack, gaps were left at the back, which

Aston Villa 0	Everton 2
	Lyons (32)
	Eastoe (36)

Ken McNaught turns away from Everton's Gary Stanley.

enabled Everton to sweep downfield whenever they chose. Indeed, the visitors went desperately close to grabbing a third goal just before half-time when a loose ball broke to Eastoe, who lashed a blistering shot that skimmed Rimmer's right-hand post. Half-time: Villa 0 Everton 2.

Villa began the second half knowing that they needed a quick goal if they were to get anything out of the game, and when they won a free-kick everyone piled forward. Unfortunately, Swain's over-hit ball into the box eluded both Evans and McNaught and drifted behind for a goal-kick. In Villa's next attack, Dennis Mortimer found Gary Shaw with a clever pass, but Gidman stuck out a boot to concede another corner, which again produced nothing.

Everton were looking more comfortable than they should have been. Billy Wright and Mike Lyons were managing to shackle Withe and Shaw to the extent that Villa's main threat had to come from another quarter. In the fifty-third minute, Villa's best chance in an age fell to Tony Morley, but the winger blasted his shot well wide from an oblique angle. Frustrated Villa now reverted to route-one tactics and speculative shooting from distance. Cowans tried a ferocious forty-yarder that sailed well over the Everton bar.

Now Villa threw men forward in a do-or-die cup-tie approach in an attempt to get back into the game, and in the fifty-eighth minute almost paid the penalty. A quick Everton break caught them cold, and they were fortunate that Wright drilled his shot wide of the post. The Toffees attacked again and again and, in the sixty-fifth minute Jimmy Rimmer had to race out of his area to whip the ball away from Asa Hartford with an expert tackle, before proceeding to jink his way round two more Everton players. He was at least thirty-five yards from his goal when he finally passed the ball

ASTON VILLA v. EVERTON

to a colleague. At least this gave Villa fans something to cheer, especially when this piece of skill set up Villa's best chance of the half. Sadly, the move ended with Cowans cracking in a low left-foot shot that 'keeper McDonagh knocked down and gathered at the second attempt.

After Des Bremner had skimmed the crossbar with a twenty-yard curler, Villa almost grabbed a consolation goal. Peter Withe headed on Kenny Swain's out-swinging centre to Gary Shaw, but Jim McDonagh dived magnificently to make a reflex save. As the game drew to a close Villa continued to press forward, and when Evans and Withe chased a hopeful cross they ended up tangled in the Everton net. Sadly the ball had been safely gathered by McDonagh, and that as they say, was that.

Two defeats in a row was a little worrying. Southampton also went down, 1-0 at Norwich. Ipswich beat Crystal Palace 2-1 at Selhurst Park to lead the table with 11 points. Southampton stayed second, but Liverpool moved into third place ahead of Villa who had plummeted to tenth.

First Division Table:

	PLD	W	D	L	F	A	PTS
Ipswich Town	6	5	1	0	12	3	11
Southampton	6	4	1	1	11	5	9
Liverpool	6	3	2	1	12	4	8
Nottm Forest	6	3	2	1	10	5	8
Arsenal	6	3	2	1	8	5	8

And now in tenth place:

Aston Villa	**6**	**3**	**1**	**2**	**6**	**6**	**7**

On 17 September Ipswich took on Aris Salonika in the first round of the UEFA Cup, winning 5-1 at home.

Aston Villa: Rimmer, Swain, Gibson, Evans, McNaught, Mortimer, Bremner, Shaw, Withe, Cowans, Morley. Sub: Williams.

Everton: McDonagh, Gidman, Bailey, Wright, Lyons, Stanley, McMahon, Eastoe (O'Keefe), Latchford, Hartford, McBride.

ASTON VILLA v. WOLVERHAMPTON WANDERERS

Football League First Division, Villa Park
Referee: Mr P.G. Reeves (Leicester)

Date: Saturday 20 September 1980
Attendance: 26,881

There was a hugely disappointing low attendance for this local derby against Wolves. Ron Saunders was forced to bring in David Geddis in place of Gary Shaw, who was suffering from an ear infection, and Terry Donovan took over the substitute's berth. Wolves' star striker Andy Gray's groin strain hadn't cleared up, so he didn't make the line-up against his former club. Gray's £1.5 million transfer to Wolves from Villa had caused considerable animosity last season. His place was filled by Norman Bell, just back from a loan spell with American side New England Teamen. Wolves made a couple of other changes. In came Hughie Atkinson in place of Peter Daniel and Colin Brazier took over Derek Parkin's number three shirt.

Villa opened up with a series of lightning attacks on the greasy Villa Park surface that had the Wolves defence back-pedalling, and it surprised no one in the crowd when Villa took an early lead with a goal that had more than an element of good fortune about it. On four minutes Gordon Cowans chipped a lovely ball to Tony Morley, who then accelerated clear before crossing low into the area. Geoff Palmer reached the ball first and booted it clear, or so he thought. Unfortunately, his clearance hit Emlyn Hughes and rebounded into the net. Villa weren't about to look a gift horse in the mouth and turned up the heat, forcing Wolves' defenders to look very uncomfortable. Almost immediately, Des Bremner raced onto a through ball to whip in a cross-shot that Wolves' goalie, Paul Bradshaw, did well to block. Villa were having a lot of joy on the right, so after five minutes Wolves' manager John Barnwell moved Berry to right-back and Palmer to left-back. Cowans caught Wolves' defence square, but Peter Withe lost his footing on the slippery surface and the ball was cleared. In Wolves' first real attack Atkinson's powerful free-kick rebounded back to him from off the Villa wall, but his follow-up lob shot flew wide. David Geddis was showing a fine understanding with Peter Withe and when he was put clear by his fellow striker Berry was forced to make a sliding tackle to win the ball.

In the fourteenth minute Wolves were unlucky not to grab a shock equaliser. Emlyn Hughes' free-kick flew off the Villa wall to Geoff Palmer on the left wing. The full-back's swinging centre sped into the box, where George Berry out-jumped the Villa defence to crash a header against the woodwork with Rimmer well beaten. Three minutes later, Villa should have gone two up. Gordon Cowans pushed a precision pass into David Geddis's run, but the striker's cross, under pressure from Berry, was put behind for a corner. Then Cowans caressed a beautiful ball to Withe, whose clever flick-on found Des Bremner, but the Scot's twenty-five-yard first-time screamer fizzed just over. Then Allan Evans put Mortimer's left-wing cross the wrong side of the post. Geddis hit a marvellous cross-field pass, of at least forty yards, to Morley, who in turn put Kenny Swain through, but Bradshaw easily gathered the full-back's tame shot. A minute later, Swain put

Aston Villa 2	Wolverhampton Wanderers 1
Hughes (o.g. 4)	Eves (69)
Geddis (84)	

Aston Villa v. Wolverhampton Wanderers

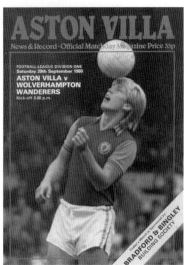

Above left: Allan Evans in aerial action.

Above right: The programme from the game Aston Villa v. Wolverhampton Wanderers, 20 September 1980.

Bremner through on goal, but Bradshaw saved the day again when he dived bravely at the Scot's feet to take the ball cleanly.

At times, Wolves' defence resorted to some over-exuberant tactics. In one incident, the referee pulled up Rafael Villazan for barging Geddis off the pitch. Villazan hotly disputed the indirect free-kick. Cowans swung the ball in, but again Bradshaw dived low to snatch the ball away from Peter Withe, who went down in a heap. However, the referee was having nothing of the striker's histrionics.

At the heart of Wolves' defence, Uruguayan international Rafael Villazan and former England captain Emlyn Hughes were just about doing enough to prevent Geddis and Withe from getting the upper hand. When Tony Morley set up the next Villa attack, Geddis held off a strong challenge from Villazan, but the striker's left-foot shot squirmed away for a corner off the out-rushing Bradshaw. As the half drew to a close, Villa's failure to score seemed to spur Wolves to the attack. Willie Carr threaded a neat ball to Hughes, who in turn found Colin Brazier, but the promising move came to nothing when the youngster over-hit his cross.

Referee Reeves seemed intent on ignoring the slippery conditions, failing to allow the players any latitude. His pernickety approach tended to stifle the game, often insisting that the free-kicks were taken from the precise spot where a foul had been committed. Right on half-time he needlessly booked Peter Withe for disputing a free-kick for impeding Villazan. Half-time: Villa 1 Wolves 0.

Snarling Wolves came out for the second half looking for an equaliser, and went close with a couple of half-chances. But as the game wore on, Villa's frustration grew more evident. Hughes and Villazan were winning the battle with Withe and Geddis, who now seemed to be out of sync with one another, often chasing after the same ball. Geddis was caught offside, a decision that rankled the crowd, especially as he ran on and smacked a shot against the post. Wolves brought on Wayne

ASTON VILLA v. WOLVERHAMPTON WANDERERS

Clarke for Norman Bell and the change brought them a deserved equaliser in the sixty-ninth minute. Clarke immediately got stuck in and put John Richards clear. His low cross flew across the Villa penalty area towards the far post, where Mel Eves raced in to side-foot the ball into the net.

Wolves continued to press forward but, twelve minutes after the equaliser, Villa regained the lead. Cowans swung in a corner with plenty of pace, and Geddis nipped in smartly to power a free header past Bradshaw. What Wolves' defenders were thinking of is impossible to say; they all left Geddis to one another. It cost their team a valuable point in a second half that they just about shaded. Wolves' spirited fightback was led by the excellent Willie Carr, who had dominated the midfield, with a string of passes to the tireless Mel Eves on the left and Hughie Atkinson on the right. Worrying for Villa was their inability to capitalise on their first-half superiority, something that Ron Saunders would no doubt concentrate on. The greasy playing surface wasn't conducive to pretty football, but with players slipping and sliding around it made for exciting stuff. The referee also booked Geoff Palmer for a foul.

The First Division table after seven league games:

	PLD	W	D	L	F	A	PTS
Ipswich Town	7	6	1	0	14	3	13
Nottm Forest	7	4	2	1	15	5	10
Southampton	7	4	2	1	12	7	10
Liverpool	7	3	3	1	14	6	9
Everton	7	4	1	2	12	7	9
Aston Villa	**7**	**4**	**1**	**2**	**8**	**7**	**9**

Compared to their rivals, Villa just weren't scoring enough goals. Next it was back to League Cup action with a trip to the seat of learning Cambridge. Cambridge were second-round conquerors of West Midlands rivals Wolves, who Villa had just beaten.

Aston Villa: Rimmer, Swain, Gibson, Evans, McNaught, Mortimer, Bremner, Geddis, Withe, Cowans, Morley. Sub: Donovan.

Wolverhampton Wanderers: Bradshaw, Palmer, Brazier, Atkinson, Hughes, Berry, Villazan, Carr, Bell (Clarke), Richards, Eves.

Cambridge United v. Aston Villa

League Cup Third Round, Abbey Stadium   **Date:** Tuesday 23 September 1980
Referee: Mr C. Downey (Isleworth, Middlesex)   **Attendance:** 7,608

This was supposed to be a dead-cert victory for Villa. According to just about every football pundit in the land, Cambridge hadn't got a prayer. So what happened? Maybe Villa thought the tie was to be played over two legs? Whatever the ins and outs of their thinking, in the end, Villa were far too casual in their approach to this game and were unceremoniously dumped out of the competition.

Ron Saunders wouldn't disclose his line-up until just before kick-off. Who would partner Peter Withe? With Geddis having scored against Wolves, Saunders had an abundance of riches. In the end Villa were unchanged, with Shaw filling the substitute's role. Cambridge manager John Docherty, who took over after Ron Atkinson had moved to West Bromwich Albion in 1978, was pleased to be able to include top-scoring centre forward George Reilly, who had recovered from a groin strain.

In the FA Cup fourth round game at the Abbey Stadium on 26 January 1980, the visit of Aston Villa had resulted in record receipts of £18,811. That game ended 1-1 with Villa comfortably winning the replay 4-1, Terry Donovan scoring twice.

The game didn't start too well for the underdogs when Villa took the lead in the sixth minute. Des Bremner won the ball on the right before pushing it to the edge of the penalty area to Tony Morley. When Roger Gibbins failed to cut out the ball, Morley took it past Tom Finney to fire a low left-foot shot past United goalkeeper Malcolm Webster into the corner of the net.

Maybe Villa were still patting themselves on the back, expecting this goal to herald a triumphant passage into the fourth round, when, just over a minute-and-a-half later Cambridge hit back to bring the score level. Right-winger Derrick Christie surged past Colin Gibson and raced towards the byline before cutting in to float the ball into the box, where Tom Finney powered in a ferocious header that Jimmy Rimmer got his hands to, but couldn't prevent the ball from bouncing into the net off the woodwork. Villa were reeling again on seventeen minutes when Cambridge scored again. Tony Morley gave away a silly foul near the left touchline and Steve Fallon's free-kick was whipped into the area. Des Bremner bravely stuck his head in the way and the ball rebounded to the unmarked Steve Spriggs, who was able to tee up the ball before smashing in an unstoppable volley that rocketed past Rimmer's despairing late dive.

Although Gordon Cowans seemed strangely out of sorts Villa came back strongly at Cambridge but, with skipper Mortimer suffering from an injury to his shoulder, were unable to penetrate United's resolute defence. Half-time: Cambridge 2 Villa 1.

The second half proved to be a bit of an anti-climax, with neither side accepting the half-chances that came their way. Villa pounded away, but time after time Cambridge 'keeper Malcolm Webster took on a 'thou shalt not pass' attitude, brilliantly palming away a couple of goal-bound headers from Peter Withe. Increasingly, Villa began to feel that this wasn't going to be their day. Tony Morley

---

Cambridge United 2   **Aston Villa 1**
Finney (8)   Morley (6)
Spriggs (17)

Gary Shaw in Japan for the World Club Championship in 1982.

just couldn't get into the game and was substituted in the sixty-third minute by Gary Shaw, but to no avail and, with Villa's frustration more-and-more evident, Dennis Mortimer was booked for dissent and Colin Gibson was booked for a foul on Christie.

On seventy-four minutes Cambridge substituted Doug Evans with Ian Buckley, and their defence continued to hold out magnificently. In front of 'keeper Webster, full-backs Dave Donaldson and Jamie Murray reduced the effectiveness of Villa's wing play, particularly that of Morley, who never looked like imposing himself on the game. United's central defenders, Lindsay Smith and Steve Fallon, just about got the upper hand in a bruising contest with Geddis and Withe, and that was it; Villa were out of the League Cup.

Villa skipper Dennis Mortimer left Cambridge with his right arm in a sling, after a nasty first-half collision with Cambridge striker Tom Finney. It was hoped that he hadn't cracked a bone in his shoulder. That he was in a degree of pain was obvious, and was definitely affected by this, particularly in the second half whenever he went for the ball. After the game Villa physio Jim Williams strapped it up, but there was extensive swelling, and that didn't look good.

Second Division Cambridge had now added the scalp of a second team from the West Midlands to progress to the last sixteen of the League Cup for the first time in their eleven-year league history with a display of aggressive power play. Villa manager Ron Saunders said that he was disappointed not to have got something from the game, and was full of praise for Villa's Second Division opponents, but added that you can't expect to win games if you let in two silly goals.

CAMBRIDGE UNITED *v.* ASTON VILLA

The blue half of Birmingham were celebrating a victory after a Joe Gallagher bullet-like header in the fifty-eighth minute had knocked the stuffing out of Blackburn Rovers.

On the following Thursday, there being no objection from the police, Birmingham magistrates lifted the drinks ban that they had slapped on Villa Park for the three home matches in October. Villa's previous two home games had been alcohol free, after magistrates refused the club a drinks licence. All bars would be open for the games with Sunderland, Tottenham and Brighton. Mr John Murray QC agreed that the previous month's refusal by magistrates was entirely justified, following another outbreak of soccer hooliganism. However, he stated that the behaviour of Villa fans was very good, also that there had been less trouble in the bars at Villa than at most other football grounds. Managing director of Stadia Catering Peter Coates confirmed that his company had provided facilities at Villa Park for ten years and that he didn't believe that sales of alcohol at the ground was a factor in hooliganism.

Fans were forced to wait and see whether skipper Dennis Mortimer would to be fit in time to play against Crystal Palace. In case his injured shoulder didn't heal sufficiently, Gary Shelton was added to the squad.

Cambridge United: Webster, Donaldson, Murray, Smith, Fallon, Gibbins, Evans (Buckley), Spriggs, Reilly, Finney, Christie.
Aston Villa: Rimmer, Swain, Gibson, Evans, McNaught, Mortimer, Bremner, Geddis, Withe, Cowans, Morley (Shaw).

CRYSTAL PALACE v. ASTON VILLA

Football League First Division, Selhurst Park
Referee: Mr D.A. Hedges (Oxford)

Date: Saturday 27 September 1980
Attendance: 18,398

Aside from the worries over Dennis Mortimer's shoulder, a mystery virus had broken out at Villa Park affecting Peter Withe, David Geddis, Jimmy Rimmer, Tony Morley, Colin Gibson and Gary Shaw, who was suffering more than most. The recommended remedy was a liberal dosing of brandy before the game. In the end they all made the starting eleven as a full-strength and top-form Villa clipped the Eagles' wings. Palace were weakened by the absence of former England international midfield man Gerry Francis.

Villa began in style, taking the game to Palace from the first whistle, and their swashbuckling style deserved a goal. In their first attack, Shaw and Cowans swapped passes, but the Villa midfielder was adjudged to be offside as he received the ball. Then a fine left-wing run by Morley won a corner that Palace cleared easily. The Eagles kept up the end-to-end stuff, with a sweeping left-wing move. Tony Sealy whipped over a dangerous cross that cool-headed Ken McNaught reached ahead of million-pound striker Clive Allen, to clear the danger. McNaught needed a bit of wet sponge treatment before being able to continue. On six minutes, Villa exploded onto the attack. Des Bremner floated a teasing cross into the Palace box that Allan Evans headed down into the path of Gary Shaw but, from only eight yards out, the youngster missed an absolute sitter, dragging his hurried effort the wrong side of the post with only 'keeper Jim Barron to beat. Palace were next to go close, and Jimmy Rimmer had to dive low to his left to keep out Neil Smillie's low shot from an acute angle. Then Allan Evans headed on to Gordon Cowans, who scrambled the ball over the line. However, referee Hedges spoiled the fun by disallowing the goal for offside.

Flanagan and Allen (not Bud and Chesney, rather Mike and Clive), combined well to create an opening for Tony Sealy, but thankfully Jimmy Rimmer was well positioned at his near post to prevent the winger from scoring. At the other end, when Gary Shaw crossed from the right, Barron decided to stay on his line but, before Withe could react, Billy Gilbert was in fast to head the ball past his own post for a corner. Barron attempted to fist away Mortimer's right-wing corner-kick, but mistimed his punch and the ball bounced off the back of Peter Withe's head towards the goal-line before being cleared.

Jimmy Rimmer was called into action in the fortieth minute to prevent a certain goal for Palace. Jerry Murphy smashed in a cannonball of a shot that Villa's goalie could not have seen until the last moment, somehow managing to dive low to his left to push the ball away. Half-time: 0-0.

Palace started the second half in determined fashion, forcing two left-wing corners in quick succession, which Villa cleared without too much difficulty. Then it was Villa's turn to attack, with a speculative ball into the Palace box that bounced dangerously near to Peter Withe and Colin Gibson, before the Palace defenders got it away.

Crystal Palace 0

Aston Villa 1
Shaw (85)

CRYSTAL PALACE v. ASTON VILLA

Colin Gibson in action.

So far Clive Allen had been kept fairly quiet by Evans and McNaught, but now the star striker came into his own. First he smashed in a wickedly swerving shot that Rimmer blocked with his legs. Then he found himself unmarked in front of goal, but failed to connect with the ball under challenge from McNaught. There was a tricky moment for Palace when Gary Shaw raced down the left before cutting into the penalty area and, although he was well tackled, the young striker managed to square the ball to Des Bremner, whose low drive from the edge of the penalty area was smothered by the diving Jim Barron.

As the game moved into its final phase Villa stepped up their efforts to snatch the winner. In the seventieth minute Peter Withe was booked for dissent, before Villa finally found the goal touch that had eluded them for most of this game. The breakthrough came in the eighty-fifth minute, courtesy of a Gary Shaw strike that wiped away the memory of his earlier miss. With five minutes to go and with his back to goal, the Villa youngster swivelled on a tanner to crash a blistering right-foot volley into the roof of the net and wrap up both points for Villa.

This wasn't anywhere near Villa's best performance to date. However, we should remember that the mark of a good side is the ability to take maximum points when falling below par. And don't forget, Villa had five players suffering with high temperatures. Ron Saunders was delighted with both points, especially considering Shaw's ear infection, and the virus that had riddled the club. He also revealed that, for several weeks, some of the younger players at the club had been suffering with chicken pox.

CRYSTAL PALACE v. ASTON VILLA

This welcome win eased Villa into fourth place in the League. Ipswich beat Wolves 2-0 at Molineux, Southampton lost, but Liverpool won 4-1. Everton were coming up fast after finding their shooting boots, having won their last four games without conceding a goal. Their last two games had been won 5-0. They now had the proud record of six clean sheets in their eight games to date. Forest were beaten 1-0 at Arsenal, and Sunderland beat Leeds 4-1 to move into the top six.

The First Division table:

	PLD	W	D	L	F	A	PTS
Ipswich Town	8	7	1	0	16	3	15
Liverpool	8	4	3	1	18	7	11
Everton	8	5	1	3	16	7	11
Aston Villa	**8**	**5**	**1**	**2**	**9**	**7**	**11**
Nottm Forest	8	4	2	2	15	6	10
Sunderland	8	4	2	2	14	6	10

Ipswich lost the second-leg of their first round UEFA Cup game 3-1 to Aris Salonika on 1 October, but went through to the next round on 6-4 aggregate.

Crystal Palace: Barron, Hinshelwood, Fenwick, Nicholas, Cannon, Gilbert, Smillie, Sealy, Allen, Flanagan, Murphy. Sub: Lovell.
Aston Villa: Rimmer, Swain, Gibson, Evans, McNaught, Mortimer, Bremner, Shaw, Withe, Cowans, Morley. Sub: Williams.

Aston Villa v. Sunderland

Football League First Division, Villa Park
Referee: Mr A.R. Glasson (Salisbury)

Date: Saturday 4 October 1980
Attendance: 26,914

Sunderland were unbeaten away from home and must have fancied their chances of leaving Villa Park with at least a point. The home side opened up brightly but soon found themselves stymied by Sunderland's dour defensive formation that was clearly designed to frustrate Villa. Tony Morley's in-swinging cross from Ken McNaught's free-kick was cleared and Colin Gibson's centre was miscontrolled by Gary Shaw. Then Morley accelerated down the left and beat the Sunderland defence with a neat chip to Dennis Mortimer, but the skipper only succeeded in lobbing the ball into goalkeeper Chris Turner's arms. Gibson put Withe through and only a desperate tackle prevented the big striker getting in a telling shot. From the free-kick, Cowans drilled a right-foot effort inches wide of the far post. Sunderland seemed content to sit back and soak up everything that Villa threw at them. The centre of their stubborn defence was marshalled by the solid partnership of big Sam Allardyce and Shaun Elliot.

An astute pass from Cowans put Morley away for a trademark run and cross that fell to Mortimer, but the skipper's shot bounced clear off a Sunderland defender's leg. Then Sunderland's best player by a street, Bryan 'Pop' Robson, swapped passes with Joe Bolton, but no other Sunderland players had kept up, and the final ball into the box was wasted. At the other end, Villa continued to pound away, but each move floundered upon the rocks of the Wearsiders' stoic defence. A strong run by Des Bremner took him to the edge of the area, before clipping over a cross that Shaw headed down to Morley, but sadly the winger's rising shot ballooned over the bar. Before the half-hour, Sunderland left-back Joe Bolton went on a strong run, swerved around a couple of Villa players, and whipped in a dangerous-looking centre that Rimmer was pleased to see Kenny Swain head clear before Alan Brown could reach it. Then it was Villa again. Gary Shaw darted between Sunderland's central defenders to tee-up Peter Withe, but unfortunately the pass was slightly over-hit. Moments later, Villa produced a move fit to grace any stadium, and it literally tore the Wearsiders' defence apart. Mortimer played a lovely ball to Gary Shaw. The youngster flicked it back into Mortimer's run, but the skipper's rising shot was inches too high. After Shaw's tame close-range header, Withe slipped the ball through to the youngster, who turned neatly before sliding a short pass to the inrushing Tony Morley. But again, the winger's exocet boomed over the bar and high into the crowd. Five minutes before the break, Dennis Mortimer floated in a free-kick that forced Black Cats' 'keeper Chris Turner to launch himself acrobatically to his right to grab a powerful header from Allan Evans. Almost immediately it was Jimmy Rimmer's turn to deny the opposition forwards with a fine leap to clutch a swinging free-kick from Kevin Arnott that was aimed for Brown's head.

Just on half-time, Villa brought tears to Sunderland eyes with a fantastic goal. Villa skipper Dennis Mortimer fought off a strong challenge to send Morley racing away down the left. As Sunderland

---

Aston Villa 4
 Evans 2 (45 & 84)
 Morley (59)
 Shaw (76)

Sunderland 0

ASTON VILLA v. SUNDERLAND

Aston Villa goalkeeper Jimmy Rimmer.

stepped up, looking for the offside, Morley beat the negative tactic by quickly swinging the ball in. Although the cross was a little behind Allan Evans, however the Scots defender produced a lethal finish of marvellous agility and skill. Despite being off-balance as he swivelled, he sent a scorching drive well beyond Chris Turner's dive for his first goal of the season. Seconds later, Villa went close to grabbing a spectacular second goal. Morley cut in from the left wing and smashed in a cannonball of a shot that beat Turner all ends up but crashed against the bar before being cleared. It was a dispirited Sunderland that trooped off at half-time, hoping that a cup of tea might help revive their shattered morale. Half-time: 1-0 to Villa.

Sunderland's second-half tactics needed to be different, but how to change a defensive-minded approach into an attacking formation when in forty-five minutes they hadn't produced more than one shot was the problem. They tried to come forward but, in doing so, began to leave large gaps at the back, which Villa punished in the fifty-ninth minute with a second goal. Dennis Mortimer squared a free-kick to Gordon Cowans, five yards outside the area. The midfielder played in Tony Morley with a beautiful through ball, and the winger made no mistake with a crackerjack of a shot that took a deflection off Gordon Chisholm on its way past Chris Turner. Sunderland hung on for grim death, not knowing whether to attack or revert to their packed goalmouth tactics. In the end they did neither. Villa sensed blood and tore into them. Tony Morley sped into the box before skimming the bar with a firecracker of a shot. Then, twice in succession, Peter Withe's misdirected close-range header was saved, and the big striker then chose to side-foot the ball, when maybe he would have been more successful with a blaster.

ASTON VILLA v. SUNDERLAND

Villa were now giving Sunderland a right royal steamrollering. However, it was not until the seventy-sixth minute that Gary Shaw grabbed the third. A great three-man move, involving Dennis Mortimer, Des Bremner and Gordon Cowans, provided a superb build-up, before the young striker latched on to the ball to caress a sublime shot beyond Turner's despairing dive.

The Rokerites had no answer to Villa's power and, eight minutes later, Allan Evans raced into the box to meet Cowan's inch-perfect corner-kick and power a header into the Sunderland net. He almost notched a hat-trick when a repeat header was well saved by Turner. Gordon Cowans and Dennis Mortimer had been superb for the entire ninety minutes and, although Villa had struggled to score in the early stages of the game, once the first goal went in there was only one team in it. Having said that, Alan Brown nearly scored with almost the last kick of the game, but the ball was booted off the line by Cowans. Villa fans went home in a delirious four-goal mood.

Since losing 4-0 at Ipswich on 30 August, Everton had been on a winning run that had hoisted them up to third place.

The First Division table:

	PLD	W	D	L	F	A	PTS
Ipswich Town	9	7	2	0	17	4	16
Liverpool	9	5	3	1	21	7	13
Everton	9	6	1	2	18	8	13
Aston Villa	**9**	**6**	**1**	**2**	**13**	**7**	**13**
Arsenal	9	5	2	2	11	7	12
Manchester Utd.	9	3	5	1	13	5	11

On Tuesday 7 October ex-Villa boss Tommy Docherty was sacked as manager of QPR for the second time in five months. The fifty-two-year-old, due to appear on perjury charges that he was acquitted of later in October, was originally dismissed the previous May, but was reinstated after supporters of the Second Division club protested. He became the sixth manager to be sacked since the season started, joining Bill McGarry (Newcastle), Alan Dicks (Bristol City), Martin Harvey (Carlisle), John King (Tranmere) and Bob Smith (Swindon). Jimmy Adamson resigned his Leeds post two months previously.

Villa had the chance to close the gap on leaders Ipswich, who were scheduled to play a League Cup replay against Norwich City. Saunders' only worry was left-back Colin Gibson, who had been injured in the Sunderland game and was substituted by Eamonn Deacy.

Aston Villa: Rimmer, Swain, Gibson (Deacy), Evans, McNaught, Mortimer, Bremner, Shaw, Withe, Cowans, Morley.

Sunderland: Turner, Whitworth, Bolton, Allardyce, Elliott, Chisholm (Dunn), Arnott, Rowell, Brown, Robson, Cummins.

MANCHESTER UNITED v. ASTON VILLA

Football League First Division, Old Trafford   **Date:** Wednesday 8 October 1980
Referee: Mr G. Courtney (Durham)   **Attendance:** 38,831

Eamonn Deacy came in at left-back to replace Colin Gibson, with Gary Williams named as substitute. Heavy rain had turned the lush green Old Trafford playing surface into a paddling pool, causing the players of both teams almost to have to try to walk on water. Despite the atrocious conditions, this was a magnificent game packed with thrills and spills. Controlling the ball was nigh on impossible for mere mortals, however these gods of football proved equal to the task, regardless of the extreme difficulties. After splashing around for a while, both sets of players seemed to come to terms with the impossibility of playing the ball along the ground, forced to rely on getting the ball into the air more than usual. It was from a Gordon Cowans free-kick in the fifteenth minute that Peter Withe rose high over the water table to head Villa into the lead.

United hit back with the equaliser in the thirty-fifth minute. Then, with a little help from referee George Courtney, they turned the game in their favour in a dramatic ninety-second spell. The referee harshly ruled that Allan Evans had handled the ball; a dubious decision to say the least. Up stepped Sammy McIlroy to send former United goalkeeper Jimmy Rimmer the wrong way. Within sixty seconds United were in front. Mickey Thomas finished a storming run down the left wing and swung over a cross to the far post, where the inrushing Steve Coppell calmly headed past Rimmer.

Lou Macari had picked up an injury and was struggling, so in the forty-third minute he was replaced by Jimmy Greenhoff. Half-time: United 2 Villa 1.

With only ten minutes of the second forty-five gone Lady Luck came definitely down on the side of Aston Villa. If the players and fans thought the United penalty had been doubtful, the one that Villa were awarded in the fifty-fifth minute was equally controversial. Kenny Swain ventured down the right and floated over a cross that the linesman decided had been handled by Kevin Moran. It was almost a duplicate of the decision against Allan Evans. The Irish centre-back was adamant, claiming that he had headed the ball cleanly. However the officials were not convinced. In both cases it had appeared that the referee was unsighted, relying on his linesman's verdict. Gordon Cowans put all distractions behind him and cracked the spot-kick to the right beyond 'keeper Gary Bailey, who dived the wrong way.

The weather gods decided that conditions weren't difficult enough for the players and sent a sudden hailstorm to make the turf even more slippery. In the fifty-seventh minute the hail stopped just in time for the crowd to get an unimpaired view of United's third goal. Sammy McIlroy found himself in space and drilled a shot past Jimmy Rimmer. In the sixty-second minute Peter Withe was shown the yellow card for crudely hacking down Nikolai Jovanovic. The pair, along with Kevin Moran, had been involved in a bruising battle throughout the game.

Manchester United 3	Aston Villa 3
McIlroy 2 (penalty, 35 & 57)	Withe (15)
Coppell (36)	Cowans (penalty, 55)
	Shaw (67)

Tony Morley.

MANCHESTER UNITED v. ASTON VILLA

In the sixty-seventh minute Kenny Swain provided another accurate right-wing cross into the United penalty area where Gary Shaw rose, beyond Bailey's despairing and mistimed attempt to grab the ball, to place a firm header into the net. Then, with eleven minutes to go, Villa missed a dream of a chance to score the fourth goal that would surely have wrapped up both points for the boys in claret and blue. Latching onto a neat through ball, Gary Shaw fed the inrushing Des Bremner, who drew Bailey off his line but squeezed his shot the wrong side of the post. Three minutes from time, Gary Shaw thought he had won a penalty when Steve Coppell looked to have knocked the ball down with his hand in the area, but this time referee George Courtney waved play on despite being well placed to see the incident.

This was a fabulous result for Villa in a contest that must have fulfilled any fan's need for excitement. It was never an easy game at Old Trafford, and this fixture was keenly contested by all twenty-two players. To come back from the despair of conceding two goals in ninety seconds was a tribute to Villa's character as well as their abundance of skill, especially considering the testing conditions. The full-blooded game was packed with incident; extraordinary refereeing decisions, unforced errors, nightmare moments of goalmouth mayhem and missed chances, plus a couple of great goals. In the end, Villa took home a point that they richly deserved, and they very nearly snatched both points. Still we shouldn't grumble, because United also deserved to take something from the game. The fans, who braved the elements, and football itself were the winners on a night when the wintry weather poured its unwelcome bounty on the players and those of the 38,831 spectators who couldn't get under cover.

In midfield, Dennis Mortimer was once again outstanding and, probably most surprisingly, young Eamonn Deacy had a marvellous game at left-back. On the last occasion this young Irishman played at Old Trafford, he had a nightmare and was substituted.

Villa were now unbeaten in their last four league games, and next up was the big one. Villa's biggest rivals had spent the previous season in the Second Division, but now the Blues were back in the big time and as anxious as ever to beat the team from the other side of Birmingham.

Manchester United: Bailey, Nicholl, Albiston, McIlroy, Jovanovic, Moran, Duxbury, Coppell, Jordan, Macari, (Greenoff J.) Thomas.

Aston Villa: Rimmer, Swain, Deacy, Evans, McNaught, Mortimer, Bremner, Shaw, Withe, Cowans, Morley. Sub: Williams.

BIRMINGHAM CITY v. ASTON VILLA

Football League First Division, St Andrews

Referee: Mr Neil Ashley (Cheshire)

Date: Saturday 11 October 1980

Attendance: 33,879

Ron Saunders named an unchanged team. The Blues were also unchanged from the side that had beaten Arsenal in midweek, Steve Lynex partnering the self-proclaimed world's biggest Elvis fan, Frank Worthington, in the continued absence of injured Keith Bertschin.

Villa were first to attack, but Tony Morley's over-hit left-wing cross flew behind for a goal-kick. Then Morley accelerated past Langan to the edge of the penalty area, only to be unceremoniously dumped on the ground by Joe Gallagher. Gordon Cowans touched the free-kick to Dennis Mortimer, whose piledriver rebounded off the Blues' wall to Des Bremner, but the Scot's scorching drive was deflected behind. Two Blues' corners in quick succession had Villa defending desperately, with McNaught coming to the rescue with a timely clearance from the second one after Rimmer had only managed to palm the ball down in the area. In the eleventh minute Birmingham almost took the lead. Again McNaught was Villa's redeemer, launching his body backwards with a spectacular overhead kick to clear Worthington's close-range acute-angle shot after it had beaten Rimmer. Worthington had become Villa's tormenter-in-chief and burst through again, with Evans happy to put the ball behind. Corner followed corner, as Blues had Villa on the rack. Their next burst forward ended with a first-time half-volley from Dillon that flew wide of Rimmer's post. Then Curbishley almost grabbed a lucky goal. Receiving the ball from another corner on the left, he left Cowans for dead before whipping in a cross-cum-shot that dipped onto the roof of the net.

After Rimmer had plucked Archie Gemmill's twenty-yard blaster out of the air, Mortimer burst through to drill in a low shot from an acute angle that Wealands did well to take at his near post. The Blues were looking fairly comfortable, but when Joe Gallagher hit a needless back-pass to Wealands from the halfway line, the off-his-line 'keeper was happy to see the ball bounce out for a corner. Cowans swung the ball to the far post where McNaught met it perfectly to smash a vicious volley that cannoned behind off Mark Dennis. The resultant corner came to nothing. However, after surviving the Blues' blitzkrieg, Villa were now having much more of the play. They won four corners in succession, until finally Worthington managed to relieve the pressure with a header upfield. But Villa weren't done yet, and Shaw smacked in a twenty-five-yarder that was only inches wide of Wealands' right-hand post. Moments later a brilliant Villa move ended with a fine cross from the right, but Joe Gallagher leapt above Shaw and Withe to head the ball clear.

In the thirty-fifth minute Villa were beneficiaries of a bizarre and controversial refereeing incident. Even the Villa players were mystified by referee Ashley's penalty decision. Dennis Mortimer whipped in a corner that McNaught met perfectly to power in a header that Wealands palmed back to him. McNaught headed goalwards a second time, where the ball looked to have been cleared by a combination of Colin Todd and Mark Dennis, but the referee's whistle halted play. At first the ref

Birmingham City 1	Aston Villa 2
Worthington (penalty, 49)	Cowans (penalty, 35)
	Evans (84)

BIRMINGHAM CITY v. ASTON VILLA

Gordon Cowans, England Under-21
v. Romania, 14/10/1980.

appeared to be signalling for a pushing offence, but actually he was pointing to the penalty spot. Apparently he had judged that McNaught's close-range header had been handled on the line. The Blues' players surrounded the official, protesting long and loud, to no avail. Up stepped Gordon Cowans to stroke the ball past Wealands to put Villa ahead.

An incensed Blues team swarmed onto the attack for the remainder of the half, but without success. Their best effort was a cross from Mark Dennis just prior to half-time. Rimmer went up for the ball amid a tangle of bodies and received a nasty bang on the head for his trouble. Half-time: Birmingham 0 Villa 1.

The second half began as it had ended, with Birmingham on the offensive, and a dangerous Curbishley cross was completely missed by Deacy, but fortunately McNaught reached it before Worthington. Villa hit back with an overlapping right-wing run by Swain, who swung over a cross that Morley headed into the middle, where Gallagher beat Withe to head clear. It was even-steven for a time, but then the Blues got back on level terms, courtesy of another dubious penalty. On forty-nine minutes Alan Ainscow tried to squirm his way through the Villa defence, but was halted by a combination of McNaught and Deacy, who appeared to have done very little other than obstruct the Blues' number seven. However, the referee had other ideas and pointed to the spot. Frank Worthington gave Rimmer no chance, and honours were even once again.

Now it was Villa's turn to be riled by the referee. Dennis Mortimer led the onslaught with a superb run from midfield to feed Morley, who crashed in a low-shot that deflected for a corner. Birmingham

BIRMINGHAM CITY v. ASTON VILLA

cleared that but Villa stormed back. Gary Shaw, the only locally born player in this derby game, went close with a fabulous shot on-the-turn that beat Wealands, but was brilliantly headed off the line by the diving Mark Dennis. Allan Evans followed this with a blistering effort from twenty-five-yards that flew just past the angle. Mark Dennis was flattened when he instinctively put his head in the way of a cannonball of a shot.

On sixty-six minutes, Morley whipped over a cross that fell to Mortimer, but again the shot was off target. The incredibly gifted Frank Worthington bemused the Villa defenders with a stunning piece of individual skill that he finished off with a tantalizing flick that fortunately failed to fool Rimmer. As the game moved into the final phase, Worthington whipped over a free-kick that Gemmill deftly headed fractionally over the Villa crossbar. Then, six minutes from time, up popped Allan Evans to break Blues' hearts with a superb volley that flew past the helpless Wealands to put Villa ahead once again. It was a shattering blow for the Blues, who in the time left weren't able to create the kind of opening that their play deserved.

The title race was beginning to hot up. West Bromwich Albion had now joined the group at the top of the table.

The First Division table:

	PLD	W	D	L	F	A	PTS
Ipswich Town	10	7	3	0	18	5	17
Liverpool	11	6	4	1	26	10	16
Aston Villa	**11**	**7**	**2**	**2**	**18**	**11**	**16**
Everton	11	7	1	3	21	10	15
WBA	11	6	3	2	14	10	15
Nottm Forest	11	5	3	3	19	10	13

Gordon Cowans played for England in the UEFA Under-21 Championship in Romania; they lost 4-0.

Birmingham City: Wealands, Langan, Dennis, Curbishley, Gallagher, Todd, Ainscow, Lynex, Worthington, Gemmill, Dillon. Sub: Givens.

Aston Villa: Rimmer, Swain, Deacy, Evans, McNaught, Mortimer, Bremner, Shaw, Withe, Cowans, Morley. Sub: Williams.

ASTON VILLA v. TOTTENHAM HOTSPUR

Football League First Division, Villa Park
Referee: Mr T. Mills (Barnsley)

Date: Saturday 18 October 1980
Attendance: 30,940

Ossie Ardiles missed this game, his place being taken by Peter Taylor. However his Argentinean teammate Ricky Villa made the Spurs' line-up, along with former Villa defender Gordon Smith, who was making a first return to his old club since his transfer to Tottenham a couple of years earlier.

Villa soon had Spurs back-pedalling as they went all-out for an early goal, but had nothing to show for it bar a series of free-kicks and shooting chances that mainly flew over the bar. On seven minutes Peter Withe earned himself a dressing down from the referee after clumsily dumping Garth Crooks on the ground. Villa's ragged early play let Spurs off the hook on several occasions. On ten minutes Spurs' 'keeper Barry Daines had to be alert to prevent Villa taking the lead. Morley fed Withe on the left and accepted a perfect return pass on the edge of the penalty area, but although he put a lot of swerve on his low shot, Daines dived to his left to smother his otherwise goal-bound shot. In the eighteenth minute Villa almost took the lead when the overlapping Kenny Swain swapped passes with Gary Shaw, before swinging in a dangerous cross. Peter Withe leapt high above the Spurs defence to power a bullet header inches the wrong side of the post. At the other end, Spurs came forward to force a save from Jimmy Rimmer at the foot of the post, with Steve Archibald racing in to meet the ball. Then Spurs' captain Terry Yorath was booked for a foul on Cowans, followed almost immediately into the referee's book by Peter Withe for dissent, after the referee had disallowed a goal for offside.

Villa got the vital breakthrough on thirty-nine minutes. Peter Withe slipped Gibson's throw-in to Morley, who darted for the box, looking at first as though he had lost possession under severe challenges from Smith and Perryman. But as Perryman attempted a back-pass to Daines, Morley pinched the ball to slide it into the net from close range. Two minutes before the interval, Villa's blushes were saved by the woodwork when Glenn Hoddle's first-time thunderbolt crashed against the crossbar from the edge of the penalty area. Half-time: 1-0 to Villa.

Villa made a fantastic start to the second half when, after only thirty-four seconds, Tony Morley was quick to capitalise on another defensive blunder. Gordon Smith could only partially head clear Dennis Mortimer's in-swinging cross from the right, and Barry Daines, who had come out to catch the ball, was left stranded as the ball fell to Tony Morley, who curled a wonderful shot beyond the 'keeper into the opposite top corner of the net. Minutes later Villa should really have gone three up following Morley's low cross-shot, which beat Daines, and flew to the unmarked Gary Shaw at the far post. But with the goal at his mercy, the youngster somehow contrived to get the ball stuck under his feet as he stumbled, and the chance was gone.

Spurs hit back and once again Villa's rather cavalier defensive tactics allowed the superb Glenn Hoddle to get in a diamond of a shot from the edge of the penalty area that needed a fantastically

Aston Villa 3	Tottenham Hotspur 0
Morley 2 (39 & 46)	
Withe (82)	

ASTON VILLA *v.* TOTTENHAM HOTSPUR

Above: Gary Williams.

Left: The programme from the game Aston Villa *v.* Tottenham Hotspur, 18 October 1980.

Aston Villa v. Tottenham Hotspur

acrobatic reflex save by Rimmer to prevent Spurs reducing the deficit. Seconds later a lightning Villa counterattack saw the ball move from Mortimer to Morley and then on to Shaw. The striker held off Lacy's challenge before hitting a shot from the edge of the penalty area that cannoned off the foot of the post. Tottenham tried to hit back, but only succeeded in leaving acres of space for Villa to exploit. However, it took several near misses before, in the eighty-second minute, they got their third goal. Daines palmed Mortimer's snap-shot to the feet of Peter Withe for the simplest of tap-ins; his first goal at Villa Park since joining the club for £500,000 from Newcastle United during the summer. It was a jubilant moment for the big striker.

This was a great Villa performance, their sixth league game unbeaten, Villa drew level with Ipswich, who were held to a 1-1 draw at home by Manchester United. With the Merseyside derby ending 2-2, Villa moved a point ahead of Liverpool and two clear of Everton.

The First Division table:

	PLD	W	D	L	F	A	PTS
Ipswich Town	11	7	4	0	19	6	18
Aston Villa	**12**	**8**	**2**	**2**	**21**	**11**	**18**
Liverpool	12	6	5	1	28	12	17
Everton	12	7	2	3	23	12	16
Nottm Forest	12	6	3	3	21	11	15
WBA	12	6	3	3	15	10	15

Meanwhile, at the club's board meeting on Tuesday 21 October, millionaire Ron Bendall was elected chairman of Aston Villa for the coming year to succeed Birmingham businessman Harry Kartz, chairman for the previous two years, who remained vice-chairman. Both stressed that the change wasn't in any way acrimonious, nor was there any boardroom intrigue at the club. Bendall, a seventy-two-year-old retired accountant, was proposed by Kartz, and held forty-two per cent of the club's shares along with his son. Villa's four-man board comprised Ron Bendall and his twenty-nine-year-old son Donald, estate agent and auctioneer Trevor Gill, plus Harry Kartz.

Villa had the chance to go top of the division for the first time in just over four years. They previously hit the top spot on 4 September 1976, but were only top for a week. That was the season the league introduced goal difference to replace goal average.

Aston Villa: Rimmer, Swain, Gibson, Evans, McNaught, Mortimer, Bremner, Shaw, Withe, Cowans, Morley. Sub: Deacy.

Tottenham Hotspur: Daines, Smith, Hughton, Yorath (Armstrong), Lacy, Perryman, Taylor, Archibald, Villa, Hoddle, Crooks.

ASTON VILLA v. BRIGHTON & HOVE ALBION

Football League First Division, Villa Park
Referee: Mr D. Webb (Sale)

Date: Wednesday 22 October 1980
Attendance: 27,367

The previous evening Arsenal beat Norwich 3-1 and WBA drew 1-1 at Everton. Once again Ipswich had no midweek league game, so Villa had the chance to go top of the table, an invitation that proved too good to miss, and they duly walloped the Seagulls 4-1 under the Villa Park floodlights to bring a smile to Ron Saunders' face after he had got off his sick bed to attend the game.

ATV had originally scheduled to show the highlights of this game, but apparently changed their minds when the Seagulls refused to wear shirts without the name of their sponsor, British Caledonian. Brighton manager Alan Mullery explained that if this had been a full televised game, his team would have worn sponsor-free shirts, but as ATV were only planning to show a few minutes of the highlights, he had decided not to bother, on the basis that Brighton's contract with the airline was worth £65,000 a year, whereas their income from TV fees was only £25,000. So nobody got to see the goals on TV. The three-year TV rights deal was reputedly worth around £2.3 million, with each club's split being decided by the football authorities.

Ken McNaught passed a late fitness test on his thigh strain in time to face Brighton's new striker Andy Ritchie. Ron Saunders was able to name an unchanged side, with the exception of Williams, who took over the substitute's berth.

Villa hit the ground running and subjected Brighton to a blitzkrieg as they powered their way to the top of the table. However, it still took them a long time to get the first goal. Indeed, before that Brighton went ahead. The visitors' resolute defence, led by Steve Foster and Mark Lawrenson, battled away to limit Villa's attackers to a couple of half-chances. The best of these were Peter Withe's marvellously controlled first-time shot on the turn that blistered the paintwork on the Brighton crossbar, and Colin Gibson's unexpected volley that 'keeper Graham Moseley palmed against the bar and caught as the ball bounced down into his arms. Gary Shaw also had a bullet-like header cleared off the line. Brighton hit back with a couple of nice moves. Then, in the twenty-seventh minute, Kenny Swain slipped as he went for the ball, allowing Gordon Smith to sprint down the wing before whipping a cross into the box where, inexplicably, Villa's other defenders had gone to sleep. In rushed ex-Villa player John Gregory to power a far-post header into the corner of the net.

Twelve minutes later, Dennis Mortimer smashed in a twenty-five-yarder that took a wicked deflection off a defender. In an incredible display of agility Moseley, who had dived in the opposite direction, jack-knifed his body in mid-air, getting his hands to the ball to turn it onto the bar. Sadly for the Seagulls, the ball bounced down across the goal line, where Allan Evans poked it home just to make sure. The linesman signalled to the referee that the ball had already crossed the line; either way it was a very welcome equaliser. Half-time: 1-1.

Aston Villa 4

Mortimer (39)   Shaw (60)
Withe (47)
Bremner (55)

Brighton & Hove Albion 1

Gregory (27)

ASTON VILLA *v.* BRIGHTON & HOVE ALBION

Spurs' Paul Miller slides in on Tony Morley in the 1981 Charity Shield.

Villa's goal machine moved smoothly into top gear and, two minutes into the second half, they took the lead. Kenny Swain atoned for his first-half slip, galloping down the right before swinging the ball over to Peter Withe, who again showed incredible control. The big striker brought the ball down beautifully and then drilled a left-foot piledriver past the helpless Moseley. Gordon Cowans and Dennis Mortimer both narrowly missed the target with shots. Then, in the fifty-fifth minute, Allan Evans split the Brighton defence to put Des Bremner clear. The Scot's first effort hit Gary Shaw and rebounded to him. This time he took deadly aim and made no mistake as his second attempt zipped beyond Moseley into the net. But still Villa's goal lust wasn't slaked and, on the hour mark, Gary Shaw slammed the Seagulls when he took Gibson's pass in his stride before pulling the trigger to beat Moseley with an excellent shot from the edge of the area.

In the final half-hour Brighton showed their mettle by refusing to lie down and die but, despite two good Andy Ritchie efforts that went close, they were mostly pegged back in their own half by Villa's mobile attack, ably led by Peter Withe. Bremner and Mortimer were tireless in midfield,

ASTON VILLA v. BRIGHTON & HOVE ALBION

allied to the beguiling skills of Gordon Cowans, who was at his impish best. Brighton really didn't stand a chance. After Swain's mistake, Villa's defence was soon back on an even keel, with Evans and McNaught having outstanding games.

Sixteen minutes of brilliant attacking football either side of half-time had completely overwhelmed Brighton and extended Villa's unbeaten run to seven league games, sweeping them to the top of the First Division above Ipswich, who had led the league table since August. It didn't matter that they had two games in hand. Both Forest and Manchester United won 2-1.

The First Division table:

	PLD	W	D	L	F	A	PTS
Aston Villa	**13**	**9**	**2**	**2**	**25**	**12**	**20**
Ipswich Town	11	7	4	0	19	6	18
Liverpool	12	6	5	1	28	12	17
Everton	13	7	3	3	24	13	17
Nottm Forest	13	7	3	3	23	12	17
Manchester Utd	13	4	8	1	19	10	16

Also on 16 points were Arsenal and West Bromwich Albion. At the bottom of the table were Manchester City and Crystal Palace with 6 points. One place above were Leicester with 7 points.

Ipswich took on Bohemians Prague in the second round of the UEFA Cup, winning the home leg 3-0.

Aston Villa: Rimmer, Swain, Gibson, Evans, McNaught, Mortimer, Bremner, Shaw, Withe, Cowans, Morley. Sub: Williams.

Brighton & Hove Albion: Moseley, Gregory, Williams (O'Sullivan), Horton, Foster, Lawrenson, Stevens, Ritchie, Robinson, Smith, McHale.

SOUTHAMPTON v. ASTON VILLA

Football League First Division, The Dell
Referee: Mr Clive Thomas (Porthcawl)

Date: Saturday 25 October 1980
Attendance: 21,249

Ken McNaught and Gary Shaw passed late fitness tests, so Saunders' only change was to name Deacy at substitute. Kevin Keegan returned to the Southampton team after missing four matches with a hamstring injury. In the first minute Southampton were dealt a body blow when Keegan went down in a crunching tackle with Allan Evans. The ex-England ace was still limping after treatment and had to be helped from the field, to return after ten minutes. The news from the dressing room was that he'd had four stitches to seal up a nasty gash on his right shin.

On thirteen minutes Mortimer touched a short corner to Cowans, who crossed to the edge of the area for Tony Morley to rifle a low half-volley past Saints' 'keeper Ivan Katalanic into the corner of the net. Saints were stunned, and inspired Villa attacked again. Ken McNaught sent a free-kick into the heart of the Southampton box, where Peter Withe out-jumped the defenders to glance a header to Evans, but the Scot took his eye off the ball as Dave Watson challenged, and Katalanic gathered easily. In the twenty-second minute Southampton pushed forward and Mick Channon fired in a speculative rising first-timer from just outside the area that flew over the Villa crossbar. Five minutes later Villa nearly scored a second goal. Morley slalomed to the left-wing byline and whipped in a vicious cross. Peter Withe beat Ivan Katalanic with a deft flick, but his clever effort was headed off the line by ex-Villa stalwart Chris Nicholl. On thirty-two minutes Swain was booked for a sliding tackle on Channon. Then, on forty-three minutes, the former England striker followed Swain into the referee's book after crudely hacking down Peter Withe. In a frenetic end to the half, Colin Gibson repulsed an all-out Saints attack with a fine tackle on Nick Holmes. With the seconds ticking away, Tony Morley attempted a rather silly pass that ended up at Phil Boyer's feet. Fortunately, Jimmy Rimmer was equal to the striker's twenty-yard drive, leaping sideways to catch the ball. There was still enough time for Ivan Golac to earn himself a yellow card for chopping down Tony Morley from behind. Then Villa had another good chance. Dennis Mortimer whipped the ball into the middle, where it was met perfectly by Peter Withe with a great close-range header that Saints' Yugoslavian 'keeper managed to scramble round the post. Half-time: Southampton 0 Villa 1.

In the first minute of the second half Southampton came forward, intent on getting the equaliser. But before Moran could reach a long through ball, McNaught darted in to head the ball back to Rimmer. Villa hit back through Withe, after Bremner had turned the ball back to the big striker but, from just outside the penalty area, his left-foot drive whizzed the wrong side of the right-hand post. On fifty-three minutes, only an outstanding reflex save by Katalanic prevented Villa from going two up. Mortimer's centre was missed completely by Chris Nicholl and the ball landed at the feet of Gary Shaw, who tried a first-time shot from close-range, but the Saints' 'keeper launched his body at the ball to save brilliantly.

Southampton 1
  Moran (60)

Aston Villa 2
  Morley (13)
  Withe (68)

Southampton v. Aston Villa

Colin Gibson.

From a free-kick, Holmes drilled in a fierce goal-bound shot that Rimmer dived athletically to push away. However, the ball only went as far as Channon, who chipped it back across goal, where McNaught headed over his own crossbar for a corner. A fifty-eighth-minute corner for Villa ended up with Evans putting the ball in the net again, but Welsh referee Clive Thomas spoiled the celebrations, indicating that he had already blown for pushing by Peter Withe. On the hour mark, Southampton got back on level terms with a brilliant move, orchestrated by the mercurial Kevin Keegan. The former England skipper surged past Cowans on the right and cracked in a high centre that Steve Moran powered into the net with a close-range header.

The goal spurred Saints into a series of lightning raids, and Jimmy Rimmer had to show his goalkeeping pedigree with some superb saves. First, he managed to get across to palm away a ferocious narrow angle shot from Golac, and followed up with a save that had a rating of ten on the difficulty scale. But then he was lucky that Moran's shot on the turn squirmed out for a corner when a cruel deflection had left him wrong-footed. Villa were still smarting from Saints' equaliser and the disallowed goal when Clive Thomas broke their hearts again. Allan Evans, on the left, chipped the ball into the box, where the inrushing Ken McNaught forced the ball over the line, but was penalised for pushing Katalanic. Despite this latest setback, Villa heads didn't go down and in the sixty-eighth minute they scored an absolute beauty of a goal. From deep in his own box, Dennis

Mortimer launched a long ball upfield to send Allan Evans racing on a 100-yard dash down the right. The Scottish defender hooked a hard low cross into the path of Peter Withe, who side-footed the ball beyond Katalanic from ten yards out. Saints' best chance of an equaliser came in a frantic goalmouth scramble, at the end of which Allan Evans managed to boot the ball to safety under pressure from three Saints forwards.

After the game Ron Saunders revealed that Jimmy Rimmer had been close to collapsing at half-time with a severe stomach upset, but had insisted on continuing. Keegan's only worthwhile contribution was to set up the equaliser. He was marked out of the game for long periods by Villa's solid defence, coupled with Dennis Mortimer's midfield masterclass. This win kept Villa on top of the table.

Ipswich kept up their challenge with a 2-0 victory at Sunderland, Liverpool dropped a point at home by drawing 1-1 with Arsenal, Forest could only manage a 1-1 draw at Norwich, Manchester United beat Everton 2-0 at Old Trafford and West Brom beat Middlesbrough 3-0.

The First Division table:

	PLD	W	D	L	F	A	PTS
Aston Villa	**14**	**10**	**2**	**2**	**27**	**13**	**22**
Ipswich Town	12	8	4	0	21	6	20
Liverpool	13	6	6	1	29	13	18
Nottm Forest	14	7	4	3	24	13	18
Manchester Utd	14	5	8	1	21	10	18
WBA	14	7	4	3	19	13	18

A report claimed that the players' bonus incentive scheme, introduced by Ron Saunders two years earlier, was costing Villa more than was anticipated. The first-team squad received £250 a point while they were the First Division leaders, which amounted to around £6,000 a week. The previous season's balance sheet revealed that four players earned between £30,000 and £35,000, three others between £25,000 and £30,000, and a further three between £20,000 and £25,000. Saunders wouldn't confirm or deny the figures, but off the record agreed that the scheme had been a factor in Villa's tremendous surge to the top of the league, and that the club's overdraft shouldn't be linked with the bonus scheme. Spiralling player wages had definitely conflicted with the recent modernisation of Villa Park and the building of the £1.5 million Holt Stand. To Saunders' credit his dealings in the transfer market had helped the club's cash flow, bringing in a profit of around £2 million over the past couple of seasons, but despite this there was a necessity to trim the playing staff still further.

On 28 October, in the fourth round of the League Cup at St Andrews, Birmingham City knocked out Ipswich 2-1.

Southampton: Katalanic, Golac, Waldron, Williams, Watson, Nicholl, Keegan, Channon, Boyer, Holmes, Moran. Sub: Rogers.

Aston Villa: Rimmer, Swain, Gibson, Evans, McNaught, Mortimer, Bremner, Shaw, Withe, Cowans, Morley (Deacy).

Aston Villa v. Leicester City

Football League First Division, Villa Park
Referee: Mr R. Bridges (Deeside)

Date: Saturday 1 November 1980
Attendance: 29,953

Before kick-off, Ron Saunders was presented with the Bell's Manager of the Month award. Colin Gibson was out with a thigh strain, Eamonn Deacy deputising. Leicester were unchanged for the third successive game, their only casualty being manager Jock Wallace, who left hospital the day before, following a knee operation.

In the first minute, the Foxes surprised Villa. Henderson robbed Deacy and played in Melrose, who lifted his angled chip over Rimmer, but the ball ran behind for a goal-kick. Then, when May's free-kick wasn't cleared properly, Villa were lucky that Smith's first-time volley was hit tamely at Rimmer from the edge of the area. Villa had started slowly and seemed happy to hit long back-passes to Rimmer.

Leicester had five men across the back in an attempt to stifle Villa's progress, and a number of promising attacks were crowded out by the Foxes' packed defence. But on fourteen minutes, Morley almost got past the visitors' defensive shield, but May was across smartly to block his twenty-yard shot. A minute later Swain overlapped down the right and crossed to the far post, where Withe powered a bullet header narrowly wide. Next minute, Withe squared the ball to Morley, whose scorching twenty-five-yarder was fisted over the bar by Wallington. From Mortimer's corner Cowans floated the ball to the near post for Shaw to get in a header that again missed the target. In the twentieth minute, Villa really ought to have gone a goal up. Larry May misjudged the flight of Evans' clearance, but Shaw dragged his low left-foot drive wide from fifteen yards. Then Cowans put Withe through after some neat work. The big striker beat Leicester's offside trap, but when he crossed low into the middle, Morley fouled May in an over-exuberant attempt to reach the ball.

On the half-hour, a neat Shaw, Withe and Mortimer combination set up Morley, whose weak left-foot shot from the edge of the area was easily gathered by Wallington. Villa really should have been ahead by this stage, especially after another display of silky skills from Cowans. However, they were fortunate in the thirty-eighth minute when Henderson swung over a swerving left-wing centre. Deacy bravely launched himself at the ball with Melrose powering in. The two players collided heavily, both needing treatment. Melrose soon recovered, but Deacy was forced to leave the field for further treatment on an injured left shoulder before eventually being substituted for Gary Williams. Moments before the interval, Henderson crossed to the unmarked Melrose, whose diving header was only inches past the left-hand post. In first-half injury time, Young exploded a twenty-five-yard dipping volley that Jimmy Rimmer plucked from the air. Half-time: 0-0.

Bad news filtered from the Villa dressing room at half-time that Eamonn Deacy had dislocated his left shoulder. Leicester were first to show at the start of the second half, when Young tried to burst through, but McNaught won the ball and laid it back to Rimmer. Villa hit back with a twenty-yarder

---

Aston Villa 2
Shaw (65)
Cowans (69)

Leicester City 0

Peter Withe shields the ball from Boro's Billy Ashcroft.

from Morley, but his poor effort ended up in the Holte End crowd. Then Morley allowed Carr a free run down the Leicester right, but Evans came to his rescue with a well-timed header. Villa were lucky when Withe gave the ball away to Henderson, but the striker fired high and wide from thirty-five yards.

Six minutes after the break, Dennis Mortimer and Gordon Cowans combined with Tony Morley on the left. But when Cowans' cross came over, Brummie-born Geoff Scott headed the ball over his own crossbar. Despite playing some good one-touch stuff, Villa still couldn't prise open the Leicester defence. Another close call came a minute past the hour mark when Morley blistered the paintwork on top of Wallington's bar with a firecracker of a shot. Three minutes later another chance went begging when Withe flicked on Williams' throw-in, but Shaw's shot on the turn flew over the bar.

On sixty-five minutes Kenny Swain whipped in a right-foot cross, and Withe out-jumped Larry May to direct the ball down to Gary Shaw, who drilled a right-foot shot past Wallington from twelve yards. It only took Villa four more minutes to extend their lead, when Gordon Cowans thumped in a great shot that bulged the back of the Leicester net. Suddenly the floodgates opened and only a last-ditch clearance by Scott prevented Peter Withe from grabbing a third goal. Scott was injured in making the clearance and needed treatment.

The game was pretty much over as a contest. However, the Foxes were lucky to keep the score to two. The referee booked Billy Gibson for a foul on Cowans and, from the free-kick, Mortimer burst down the left before sending in what looked like a perfect cross, but somehow Tommy Williams managed to whip the ball off Peter Withe's toe as he was about to pull the trigger. It was still two more points in the bag though.

Aston Villa v. Leicester City

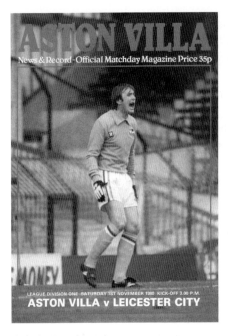

The programme from the game Aston Villa v. Leicester City, 1 November 1980.

In Suffolk, West Brom did Villa a favour by holding Ipswich to a 0-0 draw, and suddenly the gap at the top widened to three points. Liverpool could only draw 2-2 at Stoke, Arsenal beat Brighton 2-0 and Everton were held 2-2 by Spurs.

The First Division table:

	PLD	W	D	L	F	A	PTS
Aston Villa	**15**	**11**	**2**	**2**	**29**	**13**	**24**
Ipswich Town	13	8	5	0	21	6	21
Nottm Forest	15	8	4	3	26	14	20
Liverpool	14	6	7	1	31	15	19
Arsenal	15	7	5	3	20	14	19
WBA	15	7	5	3	19	13	19

On Wednesday 5 November Ipswich were beaten 2-0 in Prague in the second leg of their UEFA Cup second round tie with Bohemians, but went through 3-2 on aggregate.

Meanwhile, in a quiet corner of England, along Island Road and down a bit, it was Villa's turn to meet Big Ron Atkinson's Baggies.

Aston Villa: Rimmer, Swain, Deacy (Williams), Evans, McNaught, Mortimer, Bremner, Shaw, Withe, Cowans, Morley.

Leicester City: Wallington, Carr, Gibson, Williams, May, Scott, Melrose, Henderson, Young, Wilson, Smith. Sub: Buchanan

WEST BROMWICH ALBION *v.* ASTON VILLA

Football League First Division, The Hawthorns   **Date:** Saturday 8 November 1980
Referee: Mr J. Hunting (Leicester)   **Attendance:** 34,195

With Colin Gibson still injured, Gary Williams replaced injured Eamonn Deacy. Sixth-placed Albion would be without regular left-back Derek Statham with a hamstring injury, Barry Cowdrill taking his place, and Peter Barnes returned after missing two matches with an ankle injury. In front of Albion's biggest home gate of the season, goalkeeper Tony Godden was set to equal a fourteen-year-old club record of 182 successive first-team appearances.

The voltage of the electric atmosphere inside The Hawthorns for this crunch local derby was tweaked up a couple of notches in the opening minute with a great run down the left by Cowdrill that was only halted by Ken McNaught's well-timed tackle. Not to be outdone, Villa hit back with a run and cross by Des Bremner, but John Wile out-jumped Gary Shaw to head clear. In the ninth minute, the game was held up when around 300 Villa fans spilled from the terracing in the Woodman Corner of the Birmingham Road end of the ground. For some reason, the Villa supporters had been put in with Albion fans. After milling around behind Godden's goal for a few minutes, police escorted them to the Smethwick End to join the other Villa fans.

Villa were first to create a real goalscoring chance when Gary Shaw's overhead flick from Ken McNaught's pass set up Peter Withe for a snap header that unfortunately missed the target. This was followed by a tenacious piece of midfield battling by Dennis Mortimer earned a right-wing corner that Cowans hit low into the box, where Bryan Robson easily cleared. Albion hit back with a right-wing move involving Batson and Remi Moses, but when the midfielder shot for goal he was off balance, and the ball ran harmlessly wide of Rimmer's left-hand post. After Ken McNaught had sliced a great chance past Godden's post, a poor clearance by Rimmer fell to Cyrille Regis, who drew a great roar from the Baggies' fans with a powerful run past McNaught and Swain, but his low cross was poor.

So far there had been lots of action and promise, but not much by way of scoring chances. With so much at stake, the accent was understandably on safety first. In the first twenty minutes, both defences were in command. Disappointingly, far too many passes went astray, resulting in the game being decidedly disjointed. On twenty-six minutes, Villa might have taken the lead, when Withe headed Swain's cross down to Shaw, who found McNaught in space on the edge of the penalty area, but he ballooned his first-time shot high into the crowd.

In the thirty-eighth minute Peter Barnes, who hadn't figured much so far, cut in from the left, forcing Evans to head his swerving cross over the bar for a corner. Two minutes later, Rimmer had to get down smartly to take Brown's low first-timer at the second attempt. At the other end, it was Godden's turn to shine, keeping out a stinging twenty-yard right-foot drive from Mortimer. Half-time: 0-0.

West Bromwich Albion 0   Aston Villa 0

WEST BROMWICH ALBION v. ASTON VILLA

Gary Williams.

Villa started the second half as they had ended the first, and Wile had to be quick to take the ball from Withe as the striker burst through. Moments later, Shaw squared the ball to Withe, but the striker hurried his shot and the ball flew harmlessly over the bar. Then Godden showed great positional sense to keep out Williams' rising drive from near the corner of the area. Two minutes before the hour mark, Morley burst clear, but his ferocious twenty-five-yard low cross-shot scorched the wrong side of the post. A clever chip forward by Moses put Brown in, but a superb tackle by McNaught prevented a shot on goal. The Villa defender took a bang on the leg for his trouble, but he was able to continue without the aid of the wet sponge.

A lightning-fast break down the middle by Mortimer was halted abruptly by a crunching tackle by Wile. From the free-kick, the ball was tapped to Morley, who again confirmed that he hadn't brought his shooting boots with him by screwing the ball wide. On seventy-five minutes Mortimer burst through from midfield to whip in a blistering shot that Godden was pleased to palm over the bar. Surely someone would score soon, and it looked odds-on for Albion to do this when Moses split Villa's defence apart with a forceful thrust from midfield. But although his low shot beat Rimmer the ball flashed agonisingly beyond the right-hand post. Then, when a poorly directed ball by Evans fell to Regis, the big striker raced past McNaught before unleashing a twenty-yard screamer that whizzed a couple of yards wide.

Villa's next counterattack was ended by Wile again hacking down Villa skipper Mortimer, who was on one of his trademark sprints from midfield. However, the free-kick was wasted again by Morley, who blasted a wicked right-footer well wide from twenty-five-yards. As a spectacle, this game fell well short of meeting that objective. As an example of stifling defending and poor shooting, it was priceless. Mind you, a point apiece was not a bad result. Albion were making a habit of taking a point off the title contenders.

Arsenal walloped Leeds 5-0 at Elland Road to leapfrog Liverpool into third spot. Everton were beaten by Norwich. Meanwhile, down at The Dell, Terry Butcher was sent off as Southampton held high-flying Ipswich in a thrilling 3-3 draw.

The First Division table:

	PLD	W	D	L	F	A	PTS
Aston Villa	**16**	**11**	**3**	**2**	**29**	**13**	**25**
Ipswich Town	14	8	6	0	24	9	22
Arsenal	16	8	5	3	28	14	21
Nottm Forest	16	8	5	3	26	14	21
Liverpool	15	6	8	1	31	15	20
WBA	16	7	6	3	19	13	20

On Tuesday night, Liverpool beat Coventry 2-0 to end a run of five consecutive drawn games, Arsenal were beaten 3-1 at Southampton and Birmingham beat Forest 2-0. Best of all, Brighton beat Ipswich 1-0.

West Bromwich Albion: Godden, Batson, Cowdrill, Moses, Wile, Robertson, Robson, Brown, Regis, Owen, Barnes. Sub: Mills.

Aston Villa: Rimmer, Swain, Williams, Evans, McNaught, Mortimer, Bremner, Shaw, Withe, Cowans, Morley. Sub: Shelton.

NORWICH CITY v. ASTON VILLA

Football League First Division, Carrow Road   **Date:** Wednesday 12 November 1980
Referee: Mr T.G. Bune (Billingshurst)   **Attendance:** 17,050

Villa were unchanged. Norwich brought in McDowell at centre half in place of Hoadley.

Norwich came at Villa with an unsuspected burst of attacking football that had the league leaders in all kinds of trouble in the early stages of this match. The Canaries' spearhead of Joe Royle and Justin Fashanu put McNaught and Evans under more intense pressure than they were used to and, after a host of near-misses, almost took the lead in the eighteenth minute. Royle capitalised on a slip by Evans and, although Dennis Mortimer tried to clear the ball, he hit it straight to Graham Paddon, who fortunately dragged his shot wide. Villa managed to break out through Tony Morley, whose run and cross was headed against the Norwich crossbar and over by Peter Withe. Villa's worst nightmare came in the twenty-fifth minute when Norwich went a goal up. Mark Nightingale floated a high ball into the Villa six-yard box, where Evans fairly shrugged Fashanu off before blocking the striker's shot, but the ball ran to Paddon, who smashed it past Rimmer to put the East Anglians ahead.

The goal signalled an intense spell of pressure from Norwich, during which Ken McNaught demonstrated that he was a giant among centre halves, well worthy of a Scottish cap. Behind him, Jimmy Rimmer showed his goalkeeping pedigree. However, despite much rallying by Dennis Mortimer, Villa struggled to get going for the rest of the half. At the skipper's side, Des Bremner won tackle after tackle in both midfield and defence, constantly striving to push Villa forward. Half-time: Norwich 1 Villa 0.

Villa came out for the second half with Ron Saunders' expletives ringing in their ears, and set about answering those doubters who queried their top-of-the-table status. Ken McNaught and Allan Evans got to grips with Royle and Fashanu, which instilled a fresh confident impetus and urgency to Villa's play. After two or three dangerous attacks had provided a base to build upon, they grabbed a deserved equaliser in the sixty-second minute. The move was started when Peter Withe played a one-two with Des Bremner on the right before swinging over the perfect cross for Gary Shaw to bury his near-post header from close range for his eleventh goal of the season. Now Villa took complete control. It was as though a veil of insecurity had been lifted. Tony Morley whizzed a shot wide, and then Gordon Cowans repeated this with a shot that blistered the paintwork on the Norwich post as it flew narrowly wide. Then, in the eighty-first minute, Gary Shaw struck again to put Villa ahead. Norwich 'keeper Roger Hansbury did well to charge down a Peter Withe thunderbolt, but was unlucky that the ball ran to Shaw, who walloped the ball high into the net. Three minutes later it was all over bar the shouting. Gary Shaw turned provider when his cross from the right found the inrushing Allan Evans, who gave Hansbury no chance with a powerful downward header.

Police officers were stationed behind Rimmer's goal after Norwich fans disgustingly threw coins at the Villa goalkeeper. It was distasteful incident. But nothing could spoil Villa's delight in coming

Norwich City 1	Aston Villa 3
Paddon (25)	Shaw 2 (62 & 81)
	Evans (84)

NORWICH CITY v. ASTON VILLA

Peter Withe.

back from the brink of defeat with such an emphatic second-half display. This was a game that Norwich appeared to have under control, until it was suddenly snatched from under their noses, leaving them wondering what had happened. Once level, Villa's stuttering start was easily forgotten in a steamroller of a performance packed with craft and guile allied to hard work that simply wore down the opposition. Ron Saunders refused to get over excited about Villa's lofty perch, reportedly summing everything up with an observation regarding success: 'We are rather like a boxer after six rounds of a fifteen-rounder. We are ahead on points at the moment and feeling good, but there is still a hell of a long way to go. And, we mustn't forget the other bloke who can hit a bit as well.'

Five points now separated Villa from Ipswich, who had lost on Tuesday night. Liverpool jumped into second place. Everton won 1-0 at Leicester and West Brom were replaying their League Cup tie with Preston after two draws. This time they won 2-1.

The First Division table:

	PLD	W	D	L	F	A	PTS
Aston Villa	**17**	**12**	**3**	**2**	**32**	**14**	**27**
Liverpool	16	7	8	1	33	16	22
Ipswich Town	15	8	6	1	24	13	22
Nottm Forest	17	8	5	4	26	16	21

Crystal Palace were still bottom with 9 points, with Leicester and Brighton on 10 points.

Norwich City: Hansbury, Bond, Downs, McGuire, McDowell, Nightingale, Barham, Fashanu, Royle, Paddon, Goble (Jack).

Aston Villa: Rimmer, Swain, Williams, Evans, McNaught, Mortimer, Bremner, Shaw, Withe, Cowans, Morley. Sub: Shelton.

Aston Villa v. Leeds United

Football League First Division, Villa Park
Referee: Mr A. Read (Bristol)

Date: Saturday 15 November 1980
Attendance: 29,106

Peter Withe passed a fitness test an hour before kick-off, so Villa fielded an unchanged team, except at substitute, where Terry Donovan took over from Gary Shelton. Leeds were unchanged from the side that beat Middlesbrough in midweek.

It was raining heavily at the start of the match and, despite the protective cover having been on the pitch all morning, both teams had difficulty with the slippery surface. Then Cowans' pass skidded out of play before Morley could get to it. Then on seven minutes, Greenhoff's firm pass slid out for a goal kick. Immediately afterwards, Ken McNaught and Terry Connor needed attention when they fell awkwardly as the Villa pivot cleared the ball. In the eleventh minute Leeds stunned Villa with a goal from nowhere. Argentinean Alex Sabella cut in from the right and his stinging shot took a wicked defection to loop over Jimmy Rimmer to put Leeds ahead. Ten minutes later, Connor gave Villa's defence another anxious moment when he burst forward. Rimmer dived at the feet of the Leeds striker and McNaught managed to tidy up. Connor was hurt in the collision and had to receive treatment off the pitch. Four minutes later Villa went close to levelling the scores when Trevor Cherry brought down Gary Shaw on the edge of the area. Dennis Mortimer touched the free-kick to Cowans, who drilled a low shot inches wide of Lukic's left-hand post. On seventeen minutes, Leeds brought on Hamson to replace Terry Connor. In the twentieth minute another bone-crunching tackle by Hart left Withe limping badly.

Leeds looked dangerous whenever they broke forward but, with McNaught and Evans showing their defensive talents, Rimmer was hardly troubled. Amazingly, Hart's next vicious tackle on Withe earned nothing more than a free-kick twenty yards out. Mortimer's shot rebounded off the wall, and the Villa skipper's second attempt deflected behind for a corner. Leeds went close to grabbing a second goal just prior to the half-hour. Sabella hit a long clearance upfield that bounced in front of Rimmer and skidded off the wet surface. The Villa 'keeper, way out of his goal, somehow managed to get a hand on the ball, before gathering it in at the second attempt. Another reckless challenge by Hart dumped Peter Withe on the ground. Swain's ferocious free-kick from the edge of the area was knocked down by Lukic, who just managed to grab the ball ahead of Shaw. In the thirty-third minute Morley's in-swinging cross reached Peter Withe, who looped a header over Lukic onto the top of the net. Then two minutes later, Allan Evans tested the Leeds 'keeper with a fierce shot from thirty-five yards, but Lukic managed to scramble across his goal to push the ball behind for the corner that led to Villa's equaliser. Villa's flag-kick was only partially cleared to Tony Morley just inside the penalty area. The winger fizzed in a low shot that Gary Shaw flicked past Lukic to bring the scores level.

A minute later, referee Read booked Peter Withe for one of the most inoffensive challenges ever seen at Villa Park following Brian Flynn's theatrics when the Villa striker brushed against him. It

---

Aston Villa 1
  Shaw (36)

Leeds United 1
  Sabella (11)

ASTON VILLA v. LEEDS UNITED

Gary Shaw.

was an unbelievable booking for Withe, who for over forty minutes had been on the receiving end of some disgusting treatment from Paul Hart, including a few rather tasty, if not downright crude, tackles. Villa deserved to have gone ahead four minutes before the break. Morley raced away down the left, before whipping in a beautiful cross that Withe got to first to fire in a ferocious volley that dipped inches over the bar. Half-time: 1-1.

Villa started the second half with Kenny Swain overlapping down the right. His cross was met by Peter Withe but his header lacked real power and Lukic caught the ball cleanly. Then Gary Williams sped down the left, before swerving infield past three Leeds defenders, to crash in a fierce right-footer that squeezed wide of Lukic's post. In Villa's next attack, Withe headed the ball down to the inrushing Gary Williams, who disappointingly spooned his shot over the crossbar. On fifty-five minutes Villa almost took the lead. Tony Morley's forty-yard sprint took him through the Leeds defence before blazing a low right-footer narrowly wide.

Shortly afterwards Carl Harris beat the offside trap to crack in a terrific narrow-angle shot that flew into the side-netting. On seventy minutes Morley had another fabulous chance to score. Mortimer touched a short free-kick to Cowans, who put an inch-perfect cross onto the winger's head, but from ten yards out Morley unbelievably headed over. In another rare Leeds' forage upfield, David Hird surprised Rimmer with a fierce effort that cannoned off the Villa 'keeper's body. Then Flynn went close with a low drive that whizzed inches wide.

Villa scored what looked like a perfectly good goal in the seventy-seventh minute, when Gary Shaw put the ball past Lukic. However, the referee spoiled the celebrations by disallowing the goal

Aston Villa v. Leeds United

for handball by Withe. From then on in, the game deteriorated into a non-event, as clearly Leeds decided that one point was enough for them. The shutters went down and Villa were unable to find the spark that might ignite their efforts to grab a late and deserved winner.

Ipswich got back to winning ways after a disastrous nine-game run. Since their 6 September victory over Villa they had only taken seven points out of a possible eighteen. The Baggies took a point home from Highbury, Liverpool did the same against Crystal Palace, and Everton won.

The First Division table:

	PLD	W	D	L	F	A	PTS
Aston Villa	**18**	**12**	**4**	**2**	**33**	**15**	**28**
Ipswich Town	16	9	6	1	27	11	24
Liverpool	17	7	9	1	35	18	23
Arsenal	18	8	6	4	28	19	22
Everton	18	9	4	5	30	20	22
Manchester Utd	18	5	11	2	22	12	21

On 17 November a trio of Aston Villa players won international recognition at St Andrews, Birmingham, with England 'B' in the 1-0 win over Australia. Dennis Mortimer captained the side, and lined up with Gordon Cowans. Tony Morley came on as substitute for Cyrille Regis.

Aston Villa: Rimmer, Swain, Williams, Evans, McNaught, Mortimer, Bremner, Shaw, Withe, Cowans, Morley.
  Sub: Donovan.
Leeds United: Lukic, Greenhoff, Gray, Flynn, Hart, Cherry, Harris, Hird, Connor (Hamson), Sabella, Graham.

LIVERPOOL v. ASTON VILLA

Football League First Division, Anfield

Referee: Mr P.J. Richardson (Lincoln)

Date: Saturday 22 November 1980

Attendance: 48, 114

A massive crowd of over 48,000 screaming fans packed into Anfield to witness this top-of-the-table thriller. Villa were unchanged, with Gary Shelton taking over the substitute's berth. Liverpool had Colin Irwin in place of centre-back Phil Thompson, and Kenny Dalglish returned to partner David Johnson in attack. The reigning league champions were undefeated in fifty-nine league games at Anfield, seventy-nine in all competitions. The last side to beat them was Birmingham City in January 1978; obviously they weren't about to surrender this proud record easily.

With the strong wind at their backs, Liverpool tried a couple of long-range efforts, the first a twenty-five-yarder from Sammy Lee that zipped past Rimmer's left-hand post. Then Graeme Souness cracked in a fierce drive from twenty-five-yards that again flew wide. Kenny Swain got Villa moving with a great run that took him past Avi Cohen, but the referee got in the way of the full-back's cross-shot and the ball bounced clear. Minutes later, Evans brought down Johnson just outside the penalty area, but free-kick specialist Souness blasted the ball wide. A lapse in concentration almost cost Villa a goal. Ray Kennedy forced Kenny Swain to put the ball behind for a corner instead of getting it back to Rimmer. Then, when Lee's flag-kick came into the box, Rimmer was frozen to his line, and only quick thinking by Des Bremner prevented Kennedy from latching onto the ball. Villa continued to ride their luck in the thirtieth minute when, unbelievably, Evans decided to leave a nasty looking cross to Rimmer, who was still on his goal line. Kennedy latched onto the ball to smash a blistering drive that rebounded off Rimmer's body to Souness. The Scot should have scored but, with the goal gaping, he delayed for a split-second enabling Gary Williams to race back and hoof the ball off the goal line. Still the danger wasn't cleared, but when the ball ran to Johnson, Rimmer dived to push away the striker's stinging shot, and Morley completed the clearance.

On thirty-five minutes it was Liverpool's turn to be put under the cosh. Morley beat Neal and whipped in a low cross to Shaw. However, although the youngster's shot was beyond Clemence, Phil Neal managed to stop the ball crossing the goal line. Alan Hansen was first to the loose ball and tried to dribble his way out of the area, only to be brought down from behind by Peter Withe, the Villa striker earning a booked for his misdemeanour. The game was swinging from one end to the other and, when Jimmy Rimmer came too far out of his goal, Terry McDermott almost got through with a shot from a narrow angle, but the Villa 'keeper managed to race back to grab the ball. Then, on the stroke of half-time, Villa might have gone ahead. Shaw flicked Swain's cross into Mortimer's penetrating run, but from just inside the area, the Villa skipper dragged his shot well wide. Half-time: 0-0.

Villa were first onto the attack after the break, but Swain's cross was poor. Moments later, Dalglish turned on a tanner to beat Rimmer from close-range, only to watch helplessly as the ball squirmed

Liverpool 2	Aston Villa 1
Dalglish 2 (65 & 89)	Evans (78)

LIVERPOOL *v.* ASTON VILLA

Allan Evans.

past the post. Tony Morley had Phil Neal in a tangle again, and again the England full-back fouled the Villa winger. When the free-kick came into the box Withe fed the ball back to Shaw, who hit a scorcher wide of Clemence's left-hand post. On fifty-one minutes, Allan Evans became the second player to have his name taken after a crude challenge on Dalglish. From the edge of the penalty area, Kennedy chipped the free-kick into the box, where Ken McNaught rose highest to head the ball for a corner.

Morley was getting through a lot of good work and, in the fifty-seventh minute, Villa nearly grabbed the all-important first goal when the left winger slipped a slide-rule pass into Gary Shaw's run. With Ray Clemence out of his goal, the youngster scooped a dainty chip over the 'keeper's head but, amazingly, the England goalie threw himself backwards to palm the ball away. The Merseysiders hit back through Dalglish, who cut the ball back from the byline, but fortunately Evans was perfectly positioned to make the clearance. In the sixty-second minute a great run and cut back by McDermott was foiled by Rimmer, who needed attention to a leg injury after diving bravely at the feet of Johnson to prevent a goal. Three minutes later, Liverpool undid all Villa's marvellous work. Kenny Dalglish's dazzling run created space for a shot that the Scot swerved around Rimmer with his right foot. It was a goal of sheer class and technical finesse from the Scottish international. Liverpool, imbued by the brilliance of Dalglish's strike, pounded the Villa goal for the next ten minutes or so without success, as Villa's dogged defence held firm.

LIVERPOOL *v.* ASTON VILLA

However, one attack too many caught the Scousers out in the seventy-eighth minute. McNaught sent a long free-kick into the box that was headed out to Allan Evans, who curled a fantastic left-footer beyond Clemence's despairing dive into the top corner of the net. This was every bit as good as Dalglish's goal. Two minutes later, Villa's good fortune continued when Irwin darted into the six-yard box but, from only two yards out, he spooned the ball over the bar.

Sadly, Villa's luck finally ran out a minute before the end. Kenny Dalglish wrapped up the points for the Reds, crashing home the winner, to end Villa's hopes of taking anything from this hard-fought game. There was no time left for Villa to get an equaliser.

Ipswich beat Forest 2-1, Arsenal beat Everton, and Manchester United continued to draw. On Tuesday 25 November, Wolves did the Villans a big favour by beating Liverpool 4-1 at Molineux. This was only the Scousers' second defeat of the season, and the first time they had conceded more than two goals in a game. Also on Tuesday night Albion drew with Stoke.

The First Division table:

	PLD	W	D	L	F	A	PTS
Aston Villa	**19**	**12**	**4**	**3**	**34**	**17**	**28**
Ipswich Town	17	10	6	1	29	12	26
Liverpool	18	8	9	1	37	19	25
Arsenal	19	9	6	4	30	20	24
WBA	19	8	8	3	24	16	24
Manchester Utd	19	6	11	2	26	13	23

On 25 November Nottingham Forest won the first leg of their European Super Cup tie 2-1 against Valencia at the City Ground. The night after, Ipswich hammered Widzew Lodz 5-0 in the first leg of their UEFA Cup third round match.

Liverpool: Clemence, Neal, Cohen, Irwin, Kennedy, Hansen, Dalglish, Lee, Johnson, McDermott, Souness.
Sub: Case.
Aston Villa: Rimmer, Swain, Williams, Evans, McNaught, Mortimer, Bremner, Shaw, Withe, Cowans, Morley.
Sub: Shelton.

ASTON VILLA v. ARSENAL

Football League First Division, Villa Park
Referee: Mr N. Midgley (Salford)

Date: Saturday 29 November 1980
Attendance: 30,140

Ron Saunders named David Geddis as substitute. Other than that, Villa kept the side that lost at Liverpool. Arsenal brought in Steve Gatting at number ten in place of Brian McDermott, and with David O'Leary out, Willie Young was recalled. The hard pitch was covered with a light sprinkling of snow. Surprisingly, when the midweek cold snap had set in, the covers had not been used. Jimmy Rimmer ran out wearing a pair of black tights under his shorts to howls and cheers. It was, as they say, perishin' cold.

Gordon Cowans got Villa on the march with a great ball out to Kenny Swain, who swung over a dangerous centre that Young reached before Withe to head clear. Another piece of hypnotic skill from Cowans fed Morley, but the promising move was halted when Withe was adjudged to be offside. Both sets of players were having trouble keeping their feet on the slippery surface, and this certainly added to the excitement. John Devine felled Morley with a crude challenge, and the resultant free-kick fell to Shaw, who drilled a low right-footer narrowly wide. In the twenty-first minute, Pat Jennings had to dive smartly to his left to save Mortimer's low shot from eighteen yards. Aside from the sometimes-comical slips, the game was turning out to be a bit of a disappointment. Arsenal sat back, inviting Villa to try to break down their packed defence. Then, on twenty-five minutes, Morley swung a curling centre into the box, which Walford clearly handled. Penalty! No! Referee Neil Midgley decided that Peter Withe had pushed the Arsenal defender as he had jumped for the ball. It looked a harsh decision, especially to the majority of the partisan crowd.

Kenny Swain brought the ball out of defence with a surging run and cross that dropped to Mortimer, who slipped the ball to Withe on the edge of the penalty area. The big number nine flighted a dainty left-foot lob over Jennings, but the ball scraped the top of the bar. Tony Morley had found his feet, and his lightning breaks were giving Arsenal's defence plenty of headaches. In the thirty-sixth minute he swerved inside Devine and pushed the ball to Peter Withe, but the return pass skidded marginally out of his reach.

In the next few minutes, Villa laid siege to the Arsenal goal. Crosses and shots flew into the box, but the best chance fell to Withe just before the break. Again Morley was at the heart of the move, laying the ball into Williams' overlapping run. Villa's left-back swung in a beautiful cross to Peter Withe, who turned in agony as his powerful point-blank header was somehow blocked on the line by Walford, and the ball was booted clear. Half-time: 0-0.

Arsenal began the second half in a much more adventurous frame of mind. A fabulous ball from Alan Sunderland sent Gatting clear but, with only Rimmer to beat, Gatting's left-foot shot drifted well wide. Undaunted, Arsenal went close again when Stapleton's angled drive beat Rimmer, but skimmed the outside of the post. Six minutes after the restart, Cowans cleverly chested Swain's cross

Aston Villa 1	Arsenal 1
Morley (57)	Talbot (73)

Dennis Mortimer in action.

to Shaw, but the youngster's snap-volley flew straight at Jennings. Brian Talbot committed one bone-crunching tackle from behind too many for referee Midgley's liking. However, for some reason the ref decided that a few strong words were more appropriate than a booking. Morley was certainly looking dangerous and accelerated past Devine before crossing the ball to Withe. But the striker's left-foot shot spun tamely towards the Arsenal goal, where Jennings easily gathered. In the fifty-seventh minute Tony Morley got his reward for an afternoon of sparkling wing play. He started the move by slipping a low ball to Gary Shaw, before racing onto the return pass to crash a blistering low right-foot drive past the helpless Jennings.

Morley's next run down the left took him past one man before cutting inside Devine to hammer in another thunderbolt, but a deflection carried the ball right into Jennings' grateful grasp. On seventy-two minutes Villa might have gone two up. Again it was Villa's mercurial left winger that was the provider. On this occasion, Morley's cross was headed down to Shaw by Withe, but the young striker's first-time volley flew over the bar. A minute later, Arsenal equalised. Former Wolves starlet Alan Sunderland's low left-wing cross to the near post was met perfectly by Talbot, who glanced a deft header over Rimmer and into the net.

In the eightieth minute, Villa should have regained the lead. A high speculative ball into the Arsenal box fell to the feet of Shaw, who turned on a tanner to smack a right-foot drive inches wide of the post. Villa really should have won this game. Hopefully, this wasn't part of a trend. Two points out of a possible six was not what the fans wanted to see, despite their team's three-point lead at the top of the table.

ASTON VILLA v. ARSENAL

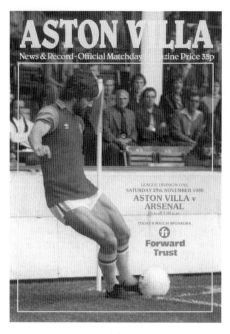

The programme from the game Aston Villa v. Arsenal, 29 November 1980.

Liverpool bounced back from their heavy defeat at Wolves to reduce Villa's lead to one point by winning 4-2 at Sunderland. West Bromwich Albion won at Spurs and Manchester United drew yet again, this time 1-1 at home to Southampton. Everton fared the same, allowing Birmingham to lift a point at Goodison Park. Ipswich increased their number of games in hand to three, as they didn't play this weekend.

The First Division table:

	PLD	W	D	L	F	A	PTS
Aston Villa	**20**	**12**	**5**	**3**	**35**	**18**	**29**
Liverpool	20	9	9	2	42	25	27
Ipswich Town	17	10	6	1	29	12	26
WBA	20	9	8	3	27	18	26
Arsenal	20	9	7	4	38	21	25
Manchester Utd	20	6	12	2	27	14	24

On Tuesday night, the Baggies drew 0-0 at Ipswich to do Villa a big favour. On the same night, Liverpool beat Birmingham City 3-1 in the quarter-final of the League Cup.

Aston Villa: Rimmer, Swain, Williams, Evans, McNaught, Mortimer, Bremner, Shaw, Withe, Cowans, Morley.
   Sub: Geddis.
Arsenal: Jennings, Devine, Sansom, Talbot, Young, Walford, Hollins, Sunderland, Stapleton, Gatting, Rix.
   Sub: Price.

MIDDLESBROUGH v. ASTON VILLA

Football League First Division, Ayresome Park   **Date:** Saturday 6 December 1980
Referee: Mr M.G. Peck (Doncaster)   **Attendance:** 15,597

Ever-present Peter Withe started his three-match suspension, so David Geddis came in for his second start of the season. Villa had gone five games unchanged, and Withe's absence was a bitter pill to swallow, considering the harsh treatment he'd endured in almost every game. The only side to have beaten Middlesbrough at Ayresome Park this season had been Birmingham, so Middlesbrough were obviously confident at home, whereas Villa's form going into this game was not exactly inspiring.

Boro started in lively fashion, hell-bent on inflicting another defeat on the league leaders. A couple of early attacks were dealt with efficiently by Evans and McNaught, and Villa's midfield trio, Bremner, Cowans and Mortimer, were forced to make a number of tigerish tackles to stub out the threat of Johnston and Proctor, along with Armstrong on the left. An impressive run by Craig Johnston was halted by Des Bremner, who took a knock that needed treatment before he was able to limp back into the action. After Rimmer had comfortably caught a Boro corner, he sent Morley racing away down the left, before the winger's run was unceremoniously ended by Armstrong. The resultant free-kick came to nothing and Boro hit back with an incisive tenth-minute move that brought Villa hearts into their mouths. Craig Johnston cut inside on the right to unleash a scorching cross-shot that beat Rimmer all ends up, but slammed against the inside of the far post before bouncing clear. One minute later Villa moved up a gear. Geddis combined beautifully with Shaw inside the Boro area before sliding the ball the wrong side of the post. Down at the other end, Cowans lost his footing as he was about to clear. The ball ran loose to Mark Proctor who looked odds-on to score. But as he swung his boot he joined Cowans on the deck, and Evans booted the ball out for a corner. Referee Mr Peck was perfectly placed to wave away Middlesbrough's shouts for a penalty.

After Geddis was booked for a wild frustrated lunge at Johnston, Boro overran Villa's defence again. Under challenge from McNaught, Proctor hit the ground like a sack of potatoes. The appeals for a penalty were even louder, but once again the referee was up with play and refused to be intimidated into awarding a spot-kick. Minutes later, Evans followed Geddis into the referee's notebook for an uncompromising tackle from behind on Dave Hodgson. Rimmer was called on to save Villa's blushes a couple of times in quick succession. First, he stopped Cochrane's in-swinging corner on the line. Then when McNaught missed Armstrong's low left-wing free-kick, the 'keeper demonstrated fantastic reflexes to snatch the ball before it could cross the line. The Boro forward's hands flew into the air, claiming that the ball had actually crossed the line before Rimmer had pulled it back. Again, the referee merely gave a slight shake of the head, plus there had been no reaction from the linesman. As the minutes ticked away to half-time, inept Villa showed a little of the attacking brio that had taken them to the top of the table. On forty minutes, Evans nodded-on a long upfield punt to the unmarked Geddis in the six-yard box. He touched it into the path of the

Middlesbrough 2	Aston Villa 1
Johnston (83)	Shaw (84)
Shearer (88)	

MIDDLESBROUGH *v.* ASTON VILLA

Kenny Swain in action against Middlesbrough.

inrushing Cowans, who was eventually beaten to the ball by 'keeper Jim Platt who dived bravely to smother the effort. Half-time: 0-0.

Whatever Saunders said at half-time certainly had a positive effect on Villa's opening to the second half. In their first attack, Geddis was floored on the edge of the Boro penalty area. The free-kick resulted in a firecracker from Tony Morley that flew just wide of the post off a defender. Then Shaw burst through, only to see Platt palm his excellent shot for a corner. Villa had come alive and, in the fiftieth minute, Geddis hit a fierce drive from fully thirty-five yards that scorched the paintwork on the outside of Platt's post. Then Mortimer threaded a lovely pass to Geddis at the near post, but the striker fired straight into Platt's arms.

The great Jimmy Greaves once told us mere mortals that football was a game of two halves, and this game confirmed his words of wisdom. Villa's skipper Mortimer went on one of his trademark runs, this time down the left, before squaring the ball to Des Bremner on the edge of the penalty area, but again the shooting boots were misaligned and he dragged his shot well wide. Suddenly Middlesbrough found their second wind, and Villa were lucky to escape scot-free when Johnston's low left-wing cross was completely missed by attackers and defenders alike before drifting out for a goal-kick. On sixty-nine minutes, Allan Evans was again Villa's saviour. Hodgson broke clear on the right, before whipping a great cross to the far post, where the unmarked Shearer powered a header past Rimmer, but Evans had raced back to cover, and calmly chest-trapped the ball, before completing the clearance. As the game moved into the final ten minutes, it looked to be heading for a no-scoring draw. Then came a mad seven-minute spell that produced three goals.

MIDDLESBROUGH v. ASTON VILLA

In the eighty-third minute, Boro made the breakthrough. Craig Johnston, in a crowd of players, stuck out a foot to redirect Hodgson's effort past Rimmer and into the Villa net. Sixty seconds later, Villa grabbed a lifeline when the linesman failed to raise his flag. Gary Shaw looked to be well offside as he received Mortimer's pass, but the young striker hared into the area on the right to hit a low shot wide of Platt's despairing dive. With two minutes to go, Boro breached Villa's defence again, with a surging left-wing run and cross by Hodgson. The centre eluded everyone except David Shearer, who slid the ball home to wrap up both points for Middlesbrough, and knock Villa off the top of the First Division. Another two points dropped!

Liverpool, who had beaten Spurs 2-1, leapfrogged Villa to lead the table on goal difference. The only team with games in hand was Ipswich who, after a 1-1 draw at Manchester City, had now played three fewer, but were only two points behind. Liverpool and Ipswich were due to face each other on the following Saturday. Villa just had to win the next one, especially considering who the opponents were!

The First Division table:

	PLD	W	D	L	F	A	PTS
Liverpool	21	10	9	2	44	26	29
Aston Villa	**21**	**12**	**5**	**4**	**36**	**20**	**29**
Ipswich Town	18	10	7	1	31	13	27
Arsenal	21	9	8	4	33	22	26
WBA	21	9	8	4	28	20	26
Manchester Utd	21	6	13	2	29	16	25

On 10 December, Ipswich lost their UEFA Cup third round second leg 1-0 to Widzew Lodz, but won the tie 5-1 on aggregate.

Middlesbrough: Platt, Craggs, Bailey, Johnston, Ashcroft, Nattrass, Cochrane, Proctor, Hodgson, Shearer, Armstrong. Sub: Hedley.

Aston Villa: Rimmer, Swain, Williams, Evans, McNaught, Mortimer, Bremner, Shaw, Geddis, Cowans, Morley. Sub: Deacy.

ASTON VILLA v. BIRMINGHAM CITY

Football League First Division, Villa Park   **Date:** Saturday 13 December 1980
Referee: Mr Keith S. Hackett (Sheffield)   **Attendance:** 41,101

David Geddis again deputised for Peter Withe and, so far, the former Ipswich striker's tally of one goal in two appearances wasn't bad. But Villa had only won once in their last six outings. Colin Gibson took over at substitute after recovering from injury. This was Birmingham's sixth successive game unchanged, but their confidence wasn't at its highest, following the previous Saturday's home defeat at the hands of lowly Leicester. Both sets of fans jammed into Villa Park, the biggest gate of the season thus far, for this thirty-eighth derby game since the end of the Second World War. The honours were in Birmingham's favour; they had sixteen wins to Villa's thirteen, with eight games drawn.

The Blues were first to show, and won a corner when Allan Evans headed Alan Ainscow's first-minute throw-in behind. Frank Worthington swung the ball into the middle, where Evans beat everybody to the ball to clear the danger. Villa broke, with Tony Morley swapping passes with Geddis, before speeding down the left wing to tee-up a half-chance for Gary Shaw, but Geoff Wealands was out smartly to push away the youngster's shot, and David Langan hoofed the ball clear. Ken McNaught's long free-kick floated into the area, where the ball was scrambled out to Allan Evans, who lifted it high into the box. But this time, Wealands made a clean catch. On ten minutes, Villa almost created a goal. Mortimer sent Morley racing into Birmingham's penalty area but Langan just managed to cut the ball out as the winger was shaping to shoot.

The commitment shown by both sets of players was typical for a Second City derby game. No quarter was given or asked for as the game developed into a rather ugly midfield battle, in which a series of bone-crunching tackles came in from both sides. In the finesse stakes, Alan Curbishley was just about shading Cowans but, at the half-hour mark, so close was this robust contest, it would have taken the wisdom of Solomon to choose between the two sides.

In the thirty-second minute, Worthington played a defence splitting pass to Ainscow, but the right winger's byline cross was easily taken by Rimmer. Not to be outdone, Geoff Wealands showed his sprinting power when he dashed out of his goal to fist away Mortimer's cross, before Geddis and Shaw could react. Two minutes before the interval, it looked odds on that Villa would take the lead. Gary Shaw controlled a fine pass, and then pushed the ball out left to Morley, who left Langan for dead, before cutting inside to smash a ferocious rising right-footer that beat Wealands all ends up, only to scorch the top of Birmingham's crossbar. Half-time: 0-0.

Two minutes after the restart Shaw had a good chance on the edge of the penalty area when Geddis glanced the ball down into his path. The young striker let fly with a left-foot piledriver that blistered the paint on the top of Wealand's crossbar. Blues had been pretty quiet since the break, but when Keith Bertschin, who incidentally had hardly had a kick in the first forty-five minutes, put

---

Aston Villa 3   **Birmingham City 0**
  Geddis 2 (64 & 83)
  Shaw (77)

David Geddis in action.

Ainscow through in the fifty-second minute, it took a well-timed tackle by McNaught to prevent the winger from getting in a shot. Then, on the hour mark, after Wealands had dived athletically to palm away a powerful header from Gary Shaw, Bertschin thought he'd scored when he pushed Gallagher's header across the line, only to turn in amazement as the referee disallowed the goal, judging that the Blues' centre-back had been in an offside position. Minutes later, Geddis swerved inside Phil Hawker to thump in a left-foot grub-hunter that Wealands was pleased to smother at full stretch. In the sixty-fourth minute Geddis finally reaped the reward he'd hoped for a minute or so earlier. Mortimer pushed the ball through into the blond striker's penetrating run where, under challenge from Hawker, Geddis drilled a low shot beyond Wealands to put Villa ahead.

There followed a bizarre sequence of incidents. Cowans swung in a cross that McNaught stretched to meet, only to be penalised when referee Keith Hackett ruled that he had been pushing. Seconds later, the yellow card was brandished, when the Villa centre-back's gentle verbal query was judged to be dissent. Then, in the next minute, a mind-numbing clash of heads between McNaught and Bertschin left both players spreadeagled on the ground. Fortunately both were able to continue after a liberal dose of the trainer's wet sponge; albeit slightly dazed. On seventy-five minutes, Mortimer slid a fabulous ball into the path of Shaw, who smacked in a stinging first-time left-foot shot that forced an equally fabulous diving save from Wealands.

Blues' manager Jim Smith needed to change things, and a minute later he took off Kevin Dillon and brought on Steve Lynex. Unfortunately for Blues, a minute later Villa went two up. David Geddis turned superbly in the box, before curling a low goal-bound shot around the diving Wealands. The

ASTON VILLA v. BIRMINGHAM CITY

ball smacked against the foot of the post and bounced back into play. Gary Shaw was first to react and crashed the ball into the empty net.

Birmingham mounted a few late attacks, but each was repulsed by the excellent Villa rearguard, and seven minutes before time Geddis nipped in smartly to slide the ball past Wealands from close-range for Villa's third. The demoralised Blues knew they were beaten, and Villa played out the remaining minutes with a comfortable game of possession football. With Ipswich sharing the points with Liverpool in a 1-1 draw, Villa were back on top of the table. Everton had staged something of a recovery to move into fifth place after Arsenal and West Bromwich Albion had both lost.

The First Division table:

	PLD	W	D	L	F	A	PTS
Aston Villa	**22**	**13**	**5**	**4**	**39**	**20**	**31**
Liverpool	22	10	10	2	45	27	30
Ipswich Town	19	10	8	1	31	14	28
Manchester Utd	22	6	14	2	31	18	26
Everton	22	10	6	6	38	28	26
Arsenal	22	9	8	5	32	24	26

Nottingham Forest lost the second leg of their European Super Cup tie 1-0 in Valencia and with it the trophy on the away goals rule, Valencia having scored in a 2-1 defeat at the City Ground in November.

Malcolm 'Big Mal' Allison was sacked by Manchester City, but was soon back in action at Crystal Palace, first of all as joint manager with Ernie Walley, and then as sole manager. And on Monday 17 November, Spurs beat Ipswich 5-3 at White Hart Lane.

Aston Villa: Rimmer, Swain, Williams, Evans, McNaught, Mortimer, Bremner, Shaw, Geddis, Cowans, Morley. Sub: Gibson.

Birmingham City: Wealands, Langan, Hawker, Curbishley, Gallagher, Todd, Ainscow, Bertschin, Worthington, Gemmill, Dillon (Lynex).

BRIGHTON & HOVE ALBION v. ASTON VILLA

Football League First Division, The Goldstone Ground   **Date:** Saturday 20 December 1980
Referee: Mr R.S. Lewis (Great Bookham, Surrey)   **Attendance:** 16,425

Ron Saunders named an unchanged side, but with Deacy at substitute in place of Gibson. Brighton blooded midfielder Paul Clark, a £30,000 capture from Southend, with Gordon Smith in the substitute's role.

Villa were on the back-foot straight from the kick-off. Geddis gave away a needless free-kick in the centre circle. Brian Horton floated the ball into the box, where Robinson stabbed it goalwards, and Morley flicked it round the post for a flag-kick. Peter O'Sullivan bent his corner under the Villa bar, where Jimmy Rimmer palmed the ball over for another corner. The subsequent clearance fell to Horton, who thundered in a twenty-yarder that forced a diving save from Rimmer. Villa won a corner on the right and, when the cross came in, the Brighton defence hesitated, allowing Mortimer to shoot for goal. The ball rebounded to Cowans, who whipped it across the goalmouth, where Brighton 'keeper Graham Moseley grabbed it at the second attempt.

Ken McNaught took a nasty knock that forced him to leave the field for attention, and seconds later Brighton swept downfield. Andy Ritchie, taking advantage of McNaught's absence, whipped in a stinging right-foot drive from just inside the area that Rimmer fielded with some difficulty. When McNaught returned, he was limping heavily. Ritchie again seized his chance, racing past the Scot, before swinging over a dangerous cross that Swain slid out for a corner. Brighton's uncompromising tackling continued, and when Cowans found Shaw ten yards outside the penalty area, Steve Foster didn't hesitate in sending the youngster flying with a crude tackle. Amazingly, no yellow card was shown, despite the referee hailing from Great Bookham. Morley hit the free-kick to the unmarked Shaw on the left of goal, who wasted the chance with poor control.

On the quarter-hour, Villa were made to pay dearly. Kenny Swain virtually gave Brighton a goal. Instead of booting the ball upfield, Villa's right-back decided to attempt a back-pass to Rimmer, but only succeeded in caressing the ball to Mick Robinson, who could hardly believe his luck. A couple of strides later, he smashed a blistering shot past the marooned Rimmer from fifteen yards.

Brighton followed up with a long-range thunderbolt from Horton that had Rimmer stretching to keep the ball out. Moments later, O'Sullivan curled a superb twenty-five-yarder around Rimmer that skimmed the top of the bar. Then Swain had to leap high to get his head to Ritchie's cross-shot. The ball ran loose to Horton, who dragged his shot wide of the post. On thirty-one minutes, Villa were in trouble again. Horton split their defence wide open with a super ball to Mick Robinson that easily beat the offside trap. The former Manchester City striker headed for goal in characteristic fashion, but a last-ditch tackle by Evans ended the danger. In a rare Villa attack, Geddis fired in a powerful right-footer that Brighton 'keeper Moseley caught comfortably, and immediately Brighton pushed Villa back into their own half once again. Horton destroyed Villa's offside-trap with a delicious diagonal

---

Brighton & Hove Albion 1   Aston Villa 0
   Robinson (15)

BRIGHTON & HOVE ALBION v. ASTON VILLA

Gary Williams in action.

ball to Clark but, with only Rimmer to beat, the young midfielder hit a first-timer harmlessly over the top.

Bremner surprised Moseley with a powerful snap-shot that bounced viciously in front of the 'keeper, the ball spilling out of his hands, before Foster booted clear. Then on thirty-six minutes, Ken McNaught's wild tackle on Andy Ritchie earned him a yellow card, as well as doing nothing to help his leg injury. Villa's play deteriorated again, with a constant stream of misplaced passes and runs into blind alleys. In the forty-first minute, McNaught's robust challenge sent Ritchie sprawling in the penalty area. Brighton hands shot in the air, but referee Lewis shook his head and waved play on. Gordon Cowans then decided to put his defence under more pressure with a stupid ball across his own box that gifted a chance to Ritchie. But with only Rimmer to beat, the Brighton striker opted for power rather than accuracy, and blasted his shot against the bar. Half-time: Brighton 1 Villa 0.

Ron Saunders delivered another half-time rollicking, and Villa started the second half with two left-wing raids by Morley that looked promising until they were halted by timely interventions by ex-Villa man John Gregory. Then business as usual was restored by Brighton. Mark Lawrenson swept through the Villa midfield and, leaving Villa skipper Mortimer in his wake, fired in a rising right-footer that skimmed the top of Rimmer's crossbar. Brighton were certainly showing Villa how to attack effectively, and any impartial onlooker would have thought that the league position of the two teams was in fact reversed. In the fifty-ninth minute, Mortimer's inch-perfect ball sent Geddis racing into the box, but Moseley was off his line in an instant to block the Villa striker's point-blank shot. Villa then embarked on a five-minute period of attempted pressure that failed to result in a clear-cut chance. On sixty-five minutes, O'Sullivan cut inside to power a fierce cross-shot that Mortimer just managed to flick off the line, with Rimmer beaten. Minutes later, Geddis was badly hurt in a challenge for the ball and he had to be carried off for attention to his injured leg. The Villa bench signalled that they wanted to make a substitution, the ref nodded, or so everyone thought. Allan Evans caught the ball some way outside the Villa penalty area. On came Eamonn Deacy, only to be stopped in his tracks by the referee, who advised that he had not stopped play for the substitution to be made and awarded the Seagulls a free-kick for handball against Evans, which thankfully came to nothing.

The game never really got going again after that bizarre incident. For the final fifteen minutes, Brighton seemed content to pull men back behind the ball and, apart from Moseley's late point-blank save from Gary Shaw, Villa failed to create anything worthwhile. Villa gave the ball away and squandered possession time after time. They ended the game with ten men, after Ken McNaught was forced to limp off towards the end. At the final whistle, both Evans and Rimmer hobbled off the pitch.

Birmingham did Villa no favours, Ipswich winning 3-1 at St Andrews, and Wolves allowed Liverpool to take both points from them to go top of the league, knocking Villa into second place. Arsenal took both points off Manchester United at Highbury, Everton and West Bromwich Albion hadn't played.

The First Division table:

	PLD	W	D	L	F	A	PTS
Liverpool	23	11	10	2	46	27	32
Aston Villa	**23**	**13**	**5**	**5**	**39**	**21**	**31**
Ipswich Town	21	11	8	2	37	20	30
Arsenal	23	10	8	5	34	25	28
Manchester Utd	23	6	14	3	32	20	26
Everton	22	10	6	6	38	28	26

Villa's faltering championship challenge was boosted by the news that star striker Brian Little would be back in the squad for the two tough Christmas games. Little had been out with cartilage problems since the previous April. So, with Peter Withe returning after his three-match suspension, Ron Saunders was able to name a fifteen-strong squad for the game against Stoke at Villa Park on Boxing Day and Saturday's away fixture at Nottingham Forest. The injury problems arising from the Brighton game had all responded to treatment, so Geddis, McNaught, Evans and Rimmer were available for selection.

Brighton & Hove Albion: Moseley, Gregory, Stevens, Horton, Foster, Lawrence, McNab, Ritchie, Robinson, Clark, O'Sullivan. Sub: Smith.

Aston Villa: Rimmer, Swain, Williams, Evans, McNaught, Mortimer, Bremner, Shaw, Geddis (Deacy), Cowans, Morley.

ASTON VILLA v. STOKE CITY

Football League First Division, Villa Park
Referee: Mr M.P. Scott (Nottingham)

Date: Friday 26 December 1980
Attendance: 34,658

Villa Park was certainly in need of a liberal dose of Christmas spirit if they were to rekindle the belief that they were good enough to challenge for the league title. Liverpool were back at the top of the table looking to make it a hat-trick of championships and, with Villa having taken only four points from their last six league games, after holding a five-point lead on 12 November, most soccer pundits began to believe that this competition was a two-horse race between the Merseysiders and Bobby Robson's Ipswich.

Ron Saunders recalled Peter Withe to lead the attack alongside nineteen-year-old Gary Shaw, with Gary Williams at left-back and Geddis named as substitute. Mid-table Stoke City had been beaten only once in a ten-league-game run that included six draws. Striker Lee Chapman had scored in each of his last three games; 11 goals in all competitions to date, compared with Gary Shaw's haul of 15. Stoke manager Alan Durban was pleased to bring back Mike Doyle for this game.

Stoke set off at lightning pace, and it wasn't long before a ball into the box was teed-up for Doyle, who drew a marvellous reflex save from Jimmy Rimmer. The Potters followed up with another incisive thrust forward that again split the Villa defence and ended with a fine effort from Brendan O'Callaghan that needed catlike agility from Rimmer to pull off a point-blank save. On the half-hour, Stoke again threatened, but Chapman was crowded out before he could reach a neat through ball.

Stoke, who had dominated the opening exchanges, suddenly found themselves back-pedalling as Villa, with Peter Withe leading the line impressively, moved up a gear. Gary Shaw powered in a bullet-like header that Stoke 'keeper Peter Fox managed to palm against his own crossbar, then Peter Withe was only inches from reaching Allan Evans' swerving centre. On thirty-four minutes, Villa looked certain to take the lead through Evans but, with only Fox to beat, the Scot volleyed inches over. The industrious Gordon Cowans was combining beautifully with Dennis Mortimer in midfield and, in the thirty-eighth minute, the ubiquitous pair created a super goal for Villa. At the end of a classic passing move, Tony Morley was sent away on the left. His cross was flicked on to Gary Shaw by Withe. The young striker flashed in a powerful header that Fox could only palm into the path of Withe, who was perfectly placed to force the ball over the line. Moments before the interval, Shaw almost had the ball in the net, but with Fox stranded, left-back Peter Hampton managed to race in to boot the ball off the goal-line. In an uncompromising first period Stoke, and Doyle in particular, were recipients of referee Mark Scott's bounty as the official frequently waved play on when another less lenient referee might have blown his whistle and spoken to the offending defenders, or even produced a few yellow cards. Half-time: Villa 1 Stoke 0.

Villa came out for the second half like an express train, and Fox had to be alert to keep out efforts from each of the Villa forwards as they cranked up the pressure on the visitor's defence. Shortly after

Aston Villa 1	Stoke City 0
Withe (38)	

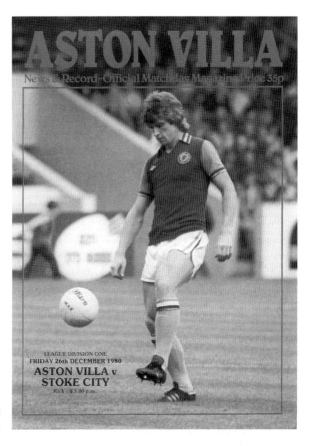

The programme from the game, Aston Villa v. Stoke, 26 December 1980.

half-time, referee Scott, who hailed from Nottingham, ignored Villa's claims for an obvious foul on Shaw, when the youngster was shoved to the ground. He then repeated this, when Doyle pushed Withe off the ball. However, the blatant fouling could not be allowed to go unchecked and, when the referee blew for a couple of fairly innocuous foul tackles in succession, he decided to book both offenders; Paul Bracewell and Brendan O'Callaghan finding their names in the little black book.

Villa were pretty much in total command of the game and, with the hour mark approaching, Evans and McNaught looked mightily comfortable against Chapman and Heath. In the sixty-sixth minute, Alan Durban threw on Peter Griffiths in place of Paul Randall, but to no avail, as Villa cruised to victory.

It was good to have Peter Withe back. He had a marvellous game and it was no coincidence that Gary Shaw produced an excellent performance alongside the Liverpudlian centre forward, who celebrated the end of his three-match suspension with his eighth goal of the campaign. We were later to hear that Withe had needed painkilling injections in his foot at half-time. Villa's delighted fans were sent home in an intensified festive mood, as was manager Ron Saunders, who was pleased with his team's performance, especially after the dismal showing against Brighton. Stoke boss Alan Durban was reported as saying that his side had lost their way after making a promising start, and had allowed Villa to take over the game.

ASTON VILLA v. STOKE CITY

Villa's victory, and Liverpool's 0-0 draw at Manchester United brought the teams level on points at the top of the table.

The First Division table:

	PLD	W	D	L	F	A	PTS
Liverpool	24	11	11	2	46	27	33
Aston Villa	**24**	**14**	**5**	**5**	**40**	**21**	**33**
Ipswich Town	22	12	8	2	39	23	32
Arsenal	24	10	9	5	36	27	29
Nottm Forest	24	11	6	7	38	25	28
Manchester Utd	24	6	15	3	32	20	27

Peter Withe, goalscoring hero against Stoke, was possibly a non-starter for the trip to Forest, joining Evans and Shaw on the treatment table.

Aston Villa: Rimmer, Swain, Williams, Evans, McNaught, Mortimer, Bremner, Shaw, Withe, Cowans, Morley. Sub: Geddis.

Stoke City: Fox, Evans, Hampton, Dodd, O'Callaghan, Doyle, Randall (Griffiths), Heath, Chapman, Bracewell, Munro.

NOTTINGHAM FOREST *v.* ASTON VILLA

Football League First Division, The City Ground   **Date:** Saturday 27 December 1980
Referee: Mr Pat Partridge (Co. Durham)   **Attendance:** 33,930

Forest weren't the force they had been were a couple of seasons earlier, when they had stormed to the league title and won back-to-back European Cups as well as back-to-back League Cups, with only Wolves halting a hat-trick of triumphs in that competition. Star striker Trevor Francis, the first £1 million player, had been missing from the Reds' line-up, suffering from a career-threatening ruptured Achilles tendon until two games earlier, when he made a goalscoring return in the 3-1 defeat of Sunderland. On Boxing Day, Forest had walloped Wolves 4-1 at Molineux. Kenny Burns was still out for Forest, but with John Robertson returning after missing four games, Cloughie was still able to field a strong team that, despite an injury hit season, was managing to keep up with the leading group at the top of the table. The previous season Villa had lost 2-1 at Forest on Boxing Day. Sadly for Villa, Peter Withe was not fit enough to face his former employers.

Villa fans turned out in force to support their team and help swell Forest's attendance to within 1,070 of its 35,000 capacity. And those travelling fans didn't have to wait long to provide a roaring vocal backing for their side, as Villa hit the accelerator from the kick-off. A high ball deep into Forest's box was headed out to the edge of the penalty area where Dennis Mortimer, wasting no time, thumped in a fierce first-timer that bounced clear off a defender. This was an altogether different Villa than had been seen in recent games. Des Bremner won a right-wing corner that Cowans swung in to the near post, where Allan Evans headed powerfully wide. Villa's next raid followed a foul on Morley on the left. Mortimer curled the free-kick into the penalty area, and with Shaw and Geddis pressing, Larry Lloyd was forced to head the ball out for a corner. Then Peter Shilton had to leap athletically to pluck Shaw's glancing header from the air.

Forest won a couple of free-kicks that were comfortably cleared by Evans and McNaught. Then Martin O'Neill weaved his way to the edge of the penalty area before scooping his effort into the crowd. Minutes later, Gary Shaw galloped down the right before slipping the ball into the run of his strike partner, but Peter Shilton was quickly off his line to boot the ball away.

In the sixteenth minute, Villa scored a somewhat bizarre goal. Dennis Mortimer forced a corner on the right, and swung a viciously curling ball to the near post, where Shilton dived low to his left to scramble the ball off his goal line. Gary Shaw lunged at the loose ball, but the swinging boot of Bryn Gunn got there first to cannon the ball against Larry Lloyd's back before it flashed past the stranded and astonished Shilton into the net.

Four minutes before half-time, Forest got their reward for a long period of intense pressure. Gordon Cowans' attempted defence-splitting pass was intercepted by Ian Wallace, who raced forward to capitalise on the space vacated by Villa's attacking midfield. The former Coventry hitman slipped the ball to the overlapping Viv Anderson, who reached the edge of the Villa penalty area, before sliding

Nottingham Forest 2	Aston Villa 2
Francis (41)	Lloyd (own goal 16)
O'Neill (86)	Shaw (68)

Nottingham Forest v. Aston Villa

David Geddis.

an inch-perfect pass to the near post, where the inrushing Trevor Francis had the simplest of tasks in slotting the ball past Rimmer. The England striker's second goal in three games sent Forest fans crackers. Half-time: Forest 1 Villa 1.

At the start of the second period Mortimer sent Geddis away on the left but, with Gary Shaw shouting for the ball near the penalty spot, the striker's cross was too close to Shilton, who gathered with ease. So far, the game had been competitive, but fair. Allan Evans changed all that with a crunching tackle from behind on Trevor Francis. Referee Pat Partridge called the Villa defender to him and, for a moment, it looked like he might be given his marching orders, but in the end his punishment was just a yellow card. Villa breathed a sigh of relief, but the City Ground crowd weren't happy, and vented their spleen at the referee and Evans.

Villa returned to the attack amid loud appeals for a penalty when Larry Lloyd appeared to control Cowans' left-wing cross with his hands. However, after looking to his linesman for guidance, Pat Partridge waved away Villa's claims. Gary Shaw and David Geddis were incensed; both firmly convinced that the Forest defender had knocked the ball down with his hand. Then, moments later,

Nottingham Forest v. Aston Villa

Villa thought they had scored a perfectly good goal. Dennis Mortimer fed Gary Shaw in the box for the young striker to crash a vicious rising left-foot drive past Shilton into the roof of the net. Villa's joy was short-lived when the officials disallowed the goal for offside; a somewhat dubious decision if ever there was one.

Martin O'Neill began Forest's next attack, speeding along the touchline deep into Villa's half, before sliding the ball to Wallace, who swung the ball over towards the waiting Francis. This time the former Birmingham superstar was beaten to the cross by Jimmy Rimmer with a timely near-post interception to tip the ball behind for a corner. Then in the sixty-eighth minute, Villa broke Forest hearts with a goal of stunning simplicity. Forest were building an attack on their left and, when the move broke down, Kenny Swain latched onto the ball and made a great overlapping run, before swinging the ball over for Gary Shaw to net Villa's second of the game.

Forest hit back with a series of attacks that brought the best out of Evans and McNaught, ably assisted by Swain, Williams and Rimmer. Villa's defence looked solid and impenetrable, until two minutes from time. A lucky break gifted Forest a second equaliser. Gary Williams looked to be under no pressure when his attempted clearance hit Carlo Ponte and bounced to Martin O'Neill on the right of the Villa penalty area. The Irish international took a step forward before drilling a low cross-shot beyond Rimmer's despairing dive.

Ipswich drew 1-1 at Arsenal and Liverpool drew 0-0 at home to Leeds. The Baggies beat Manchester United 3-1.

The First Division table:

	PLD	W	D	L	F	A	PTS
Liverpool	25	11	12	2	46	27	34
Aston Villa	**25**	**14**	**6**	**5**	**42**	**23**	**34**
Ipswich Town	23	12	9	2	49	28	33
Arsenal	25	10	10	5	37	28	30
Nottm Forest	25	11	7	7	40	27	29
WBA	24	10	9	5	31	24	29

There was now a break from league action with a trip to Suffolk to play Ipswich in the FA Cup.

Nottingham Forest: Shilton, Anderson, Gray F., McGovern, Lloyd, Gunn, Ponte, O'Neill, Francis, Wallace, Robertson. Sub: Mills.

Aston Villa: Rimmer, Swain, Williams, Evans, McNaught, Mortimer, Bremner, Shaw, Geddis, Cowans, Morley. Sub: Deacy.

Ipswich Town v. Aston Villa

FA Cup Third Round, Portman Road
Referee: Mr George Courtney (Spennymoor)

Date: Saturday 3 January 1981
Attendance: 27,721

Amazingly, the third round draw paired together two of the top three teams in the country and, with both sides at full strength, this clash of the titans promised a mouth-watering feast of football. Peter Withe's ankle injury had improved so David Geddis, who three years previously was a member of Ipswich's FA Cup-winning team, found himself back on the substitute's bench. Bobby Robson's Ipswich, unbeaten at Portman Road, were boosted by the news that George Burley was fit enough to return for his first game since November.

The players ran out onto the near-perfect Portman Road playing surface on a blustery afternoon, with Villa hoping to avenge September's 1-0 defeat handed out by Ipswich. In the fourth minute Eric Gates cleverly switched the ball to the left, where Alan Brazil swerved inside Swain to drill in a low first-time shot that ricocheted clear off Allan Evans. Then Arnold Muhren and Mick Mills fired in a couple of long-range shots, but in each case McNaught and Evans combined well to clear the danger. Next to try was 23-goal John Wark. His incredible goalscoring feat to date was 12 League, 2 League Cup and 9 UEFA Cup goals from midfield. The Scottish international let fly from just outside the area, but his effort flew well wide of Rimmer's goal.

On twelve minutes Ipswich went ahead. Dutch wizard Frans Thijssen weaved his way past Des Bremner before turning Villa's defence inside out with a fantastic forty-yard crossfield pass to Wark. He squared the ball to Brazil, who slipped a neat pass into the box for Paul Mariner to beat Rimmer coolly with a low shot from close range.

Ipswich were coping far better with the swirling wind, which was generally blowing across the pitch, rather than from end-to-end. And although Villa struggled bravely to get back on level terms, their frustration was self evident.

Peter Withe was fortunate to escape with a stern lecture from referee George Courtney when he scythed down Thijssen on the edge of the area after the Dutchman robbed him of the ball. Then, in the twentieth minute, John Wark thundered in a trademark piledriver from twenty yards that surprised Rimmer, who just about managed to throw up his hands in time to beat the ball back to the midfielder. Wark smashed his follow-up shot even harder, but the drive flew high into the crowd. In the twenty-ninth minute Allan Evans raced onto a fine cross from Gary Williams to flick a deft header towards goal that deflected behind for a corner. Cowans swung the flag-kick into the box, where McNaught out-jumped everyone to power a bullet header inches wide. In Villa's next attack, Butcher bundled over Gary Shaw as the young striker shaped to shoot, but George Courtney shook his head at Villa's appeals for a penalty, and waved play on. Undaunted, Villa attacked again and, in the thirty-sixth minute, Peter Withe turned away in frustration as Russell Osman blocked his low shot on the turn, after Cowans had teed-up the big number nine with a superb chip into the middle.

Ipswich Town 1	Aston Villa 0
Mariner (12)	

Ipswich Town v. Aston Villa

Ken McNaught takes the ball clear of Alan Brazil, watched by Dennis Mortimer and Paul Mariner.

With the interval fast approaching, Villa's defence had to concentrate on defending in numbers, as Ipswich came back at them with a vengeance. Then, from the second of two Ipswich corners in quick succession, Wark smashed a first-time volley over the bar. In the forty-fourth minute, Cooper's relatively quiet afternoon was almost spoiled when, following Mortimer's throw-in, he had to be alert to grab Peter Withe's overhead kick. Half-time: Ipswich 1 Villa 0.

Ipswich were first to show at the start of the second period but, when Mariner crossed from the left, Evans scrambled the ball away. At the other end, Mortimer's free-kick was headed down to Bremner by Withe, but the midfielder cut across the ball and his shot spun out for a goal-kick. In the fifty-first minute Villa went close to grabbing the equaliser. Des Bremner floated over a right-wing cross that dropped in front of Evans at the far post. But the defender delayed a fraction as he shaped to shoot, allowing Brazil to nudge the ball behind for a corner. On fifty-three minutes, referee Courtney booked Peter Withe after the striker had floored John Wark in the middle of the park. Another booking was not what Villa's centre forward needed, having only recently completed a three-match suspension. But two minutes later he looked to be in trouble again when a heavy collision left Terry Butcher spread-eagled on the pitch. Withe looked at the referee, who waved play on, and the big striker breathed a sigh of relief. When the ball ran out of play, Ipswich's trainer rushed onto the pitch and called for the club doctor. Butcher soon recovered, but needed a new shirt to replace the one that had been torn in the incident. As the new shirt was being donned, stud marks were clearly visible on his back.

Ipswich Town v. Aston Villa

In the sixty-fifth minute, Rimmer dived low to his left to keep out a scorching shot from Thijssen. Then, ten minutes later, an overlapping run by Williams outpaced the Ipswich defence, but his cross bobbled badly as it bounced in front of Shaw, and was cleared. The game had mostly passed Tony Morley by, so Ron Saunders substituted him with the eager David Geddis, who sprinted on to the pitch for a crack at his former teammates.

In the eighty-third minute, Villa were awarded a free-kick ten yards outside the Ipswich penalty area. The Ipswich wall formed up, and the referee booked Eric Gates for encroachment. Dennis Mortimer side-footed the ball to Cowans, who blasted in a goal-bound shot that Cooper plucked brilliantly out of the air. Minutes later, Kenny Swain combined with Dennis Mortimer to create an opening for Peter Withe, but the striker's shot dribbled tamely through to Cooper. The referee blew for time, and that was that. Villa were out of the cup at the first hurdle.

In the long run, maybe losing this FA Cup game to Ipswich would prove to be a blessing in disguise. Now Villa could quote the old adage of being able to concentrate their efforts on the league whereas Ipswich were still competing in three competitions.

Ipswich Town: Cooper, Burley, Mills, Thijssen, Osman, Butcher, Wark, Muhren, Mariner, Brazil, Gates.
  Sub: O'Callaghan.
Aston Villa: Rimmer, Swain, Williams, Evans, McNaught, Mortimer, Bremner, Shaw, Withe, Cowans, Morley
  (Geddis).

ASTON VILLA v. LIVERPOOL

Football League First Division, Villa Park   Date: Saturday 10 January 1981
Referee: Mr D. Shaw (Sandbach)   Attendance: 47,960

Villa had Colin Gibson back after missing twelve games with Gary Williams switching to substitute. With Alan Hansen still injured, Richard Money retained his place in the Liverpool side, and fit again Graeme Souness was recalled.

The game started with both teams feeling out each others' weaknesses, not the feast of football that the large crowd had anticipated. In fact, it wasn't until the tenth minute that the game sprang to life. Souness misdirected a crossfield ball that was easily cut out by Gary Shaw. The ball was touched on to Gordon Cowans, who brought Tony Morley into the play. He passed to Dennis Mortimer on the edge of the penalty area, who thundered in a rising drive that flew a few feet over the Liverpool crossbar. On twelve minutes, Johnson managed to shake free of Villa's centre-backs. He accelerated towards the area in the right channel, but Tony Morley got back to block the cross. One minute later, Morley swapped passes with Peter Withe, who fed Gary Shaw, but the final ball took a nasty hop as the youngster tried to bring it under control, and Alan Kennedy played it back to Clemence. Villa got in a couple of good attacks. First Swain's out-swinging grub-hunter bounced behind off Cowans' leg, then Shaw burst past Phil Neal, but Mortimer couldn't quite reach his cross.

In the nineteenth minute, Morley sped past Money to the byline, before whipping a fierce low ball across the box to Shaw, who turned on a tanner to smash in a first-timer that Clemence managed to beat down, and Peter Withe drilled the ball into the empty net to put Villa one-up. Villa needed no prompting to go for a second, and swept downfield again with another run and cross by Morley, but this time the officials ruled that Withe was offside. Then Withe nodded Swain's floated cross down to Shaw, and the young striker fired in an acrobatic overhead kick that rebounded to safety off Colin Irwin.

On thirty-two minutes the Merseysiders showed why they were reigning champions and top of the league. Terry McDermott burst down the wing to whip in a centre that was headed out. However, the ball fell to Ray Kennedy thirty yards from goal. The England international drilled in a ferocious low shot that had Rimmer scrambling across his goal, to push the ball round the post for a corner.

Allan Evans inadvertently gifted Liverpool with a great chance to level the scores when he slipped in the process of clearing the ball. Kenny Dalglish latched onto the loose ball, changed direction with a balletic turn, and laid a great pass to David Johnson. But with only Rimmer to beat, the striker opted for power and ballooned his shot high into the Holte End. A minute later, Rimmer had to scramble across his line to fist away McDermott's angled shot from the right after Sammy Lee had split the Villa defence with a delightful through ball. Six minutes before the break Villa hit back with some tidy work by Gary Shaw. Warding off a strong challenge, he screened the ball magnificently before laying a great pass into the path of Dennis Mortimer, who touched

---

Aston Villa 2   Liverpool 0
  Withe (19)
  Mortimer (82)

ASTON VILLA v. LIVERPOOL

Dennis Mortimer shows off the league championship trophy at the start of season 1981/82.

the ball to Withe but, as the striker was about to pull the trigger, a superb tackle pushed the ball out for a corner.

In the forty-second minute, Souness fired a venomous shot narrowly wide. Then, seconds before the interval, Shaw's clever step-over put Mortimer clear. The Villa skipper fed the ball left to Morley who swerved inside to crash in a cross-cum-shot that Irwin was pleased to head clear. Half-time: Villa 1 Liverpool 0.

Liverpool started the second-period with a couple of enterprising attacks and, in the forty-ninth minute, Des Bremner stopped Alan Kennedy's run unfairly. Souness touched the ball to McDermott, whose rising drive, from eight yards outside the penalty area, flew high and wide. Near the hour mark, Kenny Dalglish burst forward, for once escaping the close attentions of Ken McNaught, but his shot, from an acute angle, was booted clear by Kenny Swain. Then referee Shaw, no relation to Gary, put a dampener on a marvellous performance by showing McNaught the yellow card after the Scot had seemed to win the ball cleanly in a tackle on Johnson. To add insult to injury, seconds later, the referee mystifyingly ignored a much worse foul by Kenny Swain, when he floored Alan Kennedy, and simply awarded a free-kick to the Scousers. Allan Evans, and then Withe, came to Villa's rescue to concede corners with timely headers in dangerous situations.

In the final ten minutes of the game Villa emerged from a real grilling to mount a number of attacking moves that would eventually lead to a second goal. First, Allan Evans ran through unimpeded to exchange passes with Gary Shaw before lining up a shot that drifted a couple of feet wide. In the eighty-second minute Kenny Swain took off on a characteristic run before finding

Gary Shaw in space. The youngster shielded the ball magnificently before slipping a slide-rule pass into the run of Mortimer, whose intelligent burst into the heart of the area ended with him drawing Clemence off his line and coolly sliding the ball beyond his despairing dive into the corner of the net. It was a goal fit to grace any of the world's top stadiums.

Liverpool tried to come back but McNaught and Evans simply didn't allow them any space at all. The referee's whistle brought to an end an absorbing contest between two heavyweights of the First Division. This win took Villa back to the top of the table, dropping Liverpool from first place to third. It was time for even the most negative of pundits to acclaim Villa as worthy contenders for the title.

Ipswich beat Forest 2-0 to leapfrog the Merseysiders into second spot. Manchester United, West Bromwich Albion and Arsenal also won.

The First Division table:

	PLD	W	D	L	F	A	PTS
Aston Villa	**26**	**15**	**6**	**5**	**44**	**23**	**36**
Ipswich Town	24	13	9	2	42	21	35
Liverpool	26	11	12	3	46	29	34
Arsenal	26	11	10	5	39	29	32
WBA	25	11	9	5	33	24	31
Nottm Forest	26	11	7	8	40	29	29

Sadly, Villa's lead at the top was short-lived. On Tuesday night, 13 January, Ipswich beat Forest 2-0 at home to regain top spot for the first time since 24 October. On 14 January, Liverpool beat Manchester City 1-0 at Maine Road in the first leg of their League Cup semi-final.

Aston Villa: Rimmer, Swain, Gibson, Evans, McNaught, Mortimer, Bremner, Shaw, Withe, Cowans, Morley. Sub: Williams.

Liverpool: Clemence, Neal, Kennedy A., Irwin, Kennedy R., Money, Dalglish, Lee, Johnson, McDermott, Souness. Sub: Case.

COVENTRY CITY v. ASTON VILLA

Football League First Division, Highfield Road   **Date:** Saturday 17 January 1981
Referee: Mr K.G. Salmon (Barnet)   **Attendance:** 27,020

Villa were unchanged for this game. Coventry had striker Mick Ferguson back, after passing a late fitness test on his injured ankle. The fans hoped that Villa would continue their winning ways, but before the game was one minute old, Coventry almost caught them cold. Les Sealey sent a huge kick deep into Villa territory and Garry Thompson rose highest to nod the ball down to Ferguson, but Colin Gibson was onto it in a flash to prod the ball back to Jimmy Rimmer. In the seventh minute, Kenny Swain floated a free-kick to the far post, where Allan Evans failed to react quickly enough, allowing Mick Coop to get the ball clear. Then Coventry won a corner, which Andy Blair swung into the middle and, in a lively melee, Thompson and McNaught were hurt before Kenny Swain booted the ball clear. It took a few minutes of treatment before McNaught was able to resume. When the ball went dead from Coventry's next attack, Ferguson wanted a corner, but referee Salmon awarded a goal-kick to Villa. To show his displeasure, Ferguson slammed the ball to the ground, and was lucky to escape with a lecture rather than a yellow card.

On seventeen minutes, the Sky Blues won a free-kick just outside the penalty area, which Brian 'Harry' Roberts blasted at the Villa wall. The ball rebounded to Thompson, who sent a dipping volley just past Rimmer's right-hand post. Referee Salmon again showed considerable leniency, by not booking McNaught for a bone-crunching tackle on Ferguson. This wasn't the first tasty challenge by any means, but with the referee allowing plenty of latitude, the players couldn't be blamed for their over-exuberance.

Just after the half-hour, Allan Evans surged onto the offensive, with a powerful lung-bursting run from deep. His venomous low shot ricocheted to Gary Shaw off Dennis Mortimer, and the young striker drew a fantastic flying save from Les Sealey with a left-foot thunderbolt. Then, thirty seconds later, the referee decided he'd had enough of the rough stuff and showed the yellow card to Colin Gibson for a nasty late tackle on Danny Thomas. Moves involving three passes or more were as scarce as rocking-horse droppings, but occasionally the dull routine was broken by a flash of skill.

Following another lengthy wrestling match with McNaught, the referee pulled Ferguson to one side and delivered a stern lecture. With half-time fast approaching, Villa stormed on to the attack. Peter Withe sprinted onto a lovely pass, before back-heeling the ball to Tony Morley, who smashed in a scorching drive that shook Sealey's right-hand post and spun behind for a goal-kick. Seconds later, Gary Gillespie upended Gary Shaw just outside the Sky Blues' penalty area. Mortimer tapped the free-kick to Gordon Cowans, who hit a right-foot screamer that scorched the paint off the outside of Sealey's left-hand post. Half-time: 0-0.

Villa began the second half began with three quick corners, and on two separate occasions Withe and Shaw forced Sealey to race off his line to boot the ball clear. In the fifty-second minute, Dennis

Coventry City 1	Aston Villa 2
Hateley (71)	Morley (55)
	Withe (65)

COVENTRY CITY v. ASTON VILLA

Villa's Peter Withe in action for England against Scotland.

Mortimer swapped passes with Shaw before drilling a low shot that Sealey dived to smother. Two minutes later, Villa should really have won a penalty. Roberts miskicked Morley's left-wing cross and launched a crazy tackle on Bremner from behind as the Villa midfielder shaped to shoot. How the referee failed to give a penalty was absolutely amazing. The official merely shook his head and waved play on. An incensed Villa stormed back to the attack, and a minute later justice was done. Morley accelerated down the left wing and swerved inside Coop to smash in a vicious drive that flew past the helpless Sealey to give Villa a deserved lead.

The linesman running the half that Villa were attacking had already stopped a number of promising attacks. Now he did it again. Bremner surged past a couple of Coventry players before pushing a slide-rule pass to Shaw, who was clearly onside when he raced through, but the linesman raised his flag again to end a lovely move. Mortimer and Shaw combined well to set up a shooting chance for Kenny Swain, but Sealey got down well to smother his tight-angled shot. At the other end, Ferguson swivelled on the eighteen-yard line to smash in a wicked drive that bounced off McNaught for a corner. The big striker was substituted in the sixty-fourth minute for Mark Hateley. One minute later, Villa extended their lead with a hotly disputed goal. Morley got down the left and centred to the unmarked Peter Withe, who glanced a deft header past Sealey. Coventry claimed offside but, for once, the linesman disagreed and the goal stood. Villa wanted a third but, Sealey easily gathered Shaw's tame shot. Then Gillespie pulled Gibson to the ground before he could shoot. Cowans whipped the resultant free-kick into the box with power and pace, and Paul Dyson was

COVENTRY CITY v. ASTON VILLA

happy to nod the ball over the crossbar for a corner. Coventry came back strongly, and scored in the seventy-first minute.

Former Villa man Steve Hunt swung in a free-kick that was met powerfully by Mark Hateley, who leaped high above the Villa defence to flight a bullet header past Rimmer. Danny Thomas was booked for hacking down Dennis Mortimer, then Steve Hunt's first-timer flew off Gibson for a corner. And with Hateley and Dyson challenging, Peter Withe headed the ball off the goal line. Thompson wasted a great chance in the eighty-first minute when Daly's corner fell to him and he fired a rising close-range shot the wrong side of the post. Despite Coventry's best efforts, Villa hung on to win with a display of resolute defending.

Ipswich drew 0-0 at Everton, Liverpool won 1-0 at Norwich, Arsenal lost 2-0 at Tottenham and West Bromwich Albion beat Brighton 2-0.

The First Division table:

	PLD	W	D	L	F	A	PTS
Ipswich Town	26	14	10	2	47	22	38
Aston Villa	**27**	**16**	**6**	**5**	**46**	**24**	**38**
Liverpool	27	12	12	3	47	29	36
WBA	26	12	9	5	35	24	33
Arsenal	27	11	10	6	39	31	32
Southampton	27	12	7	8	54	40	31

On Monday 19 January, the earlier decision by the FA Council to end the system of yellow and red cards came into force. This ruling was to be applied in all English leagues and other competitions, as well as friendly games.

Saturday 24 January, was the fourth round of the FA Cup, and as Villa had been knocked out in the third round, they had no game. Here are a few interesting results: Coventry beat Birmingham 3-0, Everton beat Liverpool 2-1, Middlesbrough beat West Bromwich Albion 1-0, Forest beat Manchester United 1-0 and Ipswich drew 0-0 at Shrewsbury. Then on Tuesday 27 January, Coventry City beat West Ham 3-2 at Highfield Road in the first leg of the other League Cup semi-final, and Ipswich beat Shrewsbury 3-0 in their FA Cup fourth round replay.

Coventry City: Sealey, Coop, Roberts, Blair, Dyson, Gillespie, Thomas, Daly, Thompson, Ferguson (Hateley), Hunt.

Aston Villa: Rimmer, Swain, Gibson, Evans, McNaught, Mortimer, Bremner, Shaw, Withe, Cowans, Morley. Sub: Williams.

ASTON VILLA v. MANCHESTER CITY

Football League First Division, Villa Park

Referee: Mr B.T. Stevens (Stonehouse, Glos)

Date: Saturday 31 January 1981

Attendance: 33,682

Ron Saunders brought in young Irishman Eamonn Deacy at left-back in place of Gibson, with Geddis on the bench instead of Williams. Unbeaten in their last five league games, John Bond's City had Dave Bennett at number seven in place of Phil Boyer, City's £220,000 November capture from Southampton, Tony Henry at right-back in place of Ranson and Tommy Booth in for Reid at number four. City had former Villa man Bobby McDonald at left-back. Bond had taken over the manager's reins at City in October after big-spending Malcolm Allison had been sacked.

On two minutes, Villa got an early breakthrough. Peter Withe threw his body backwards, sending an overhead kick across the area to Allan Evans. He nodded the ball to the inrushing Gary Shaw, who volleyed into the roof of the net from six yards. Jimmy Rimmer had to be alert to keep out good efforts from Steve Mackenzie and Paul Power. Then a mistake by Gerry Gow let in Peter Withe, who raced forward before delivering an inch-perfect pass for Gary Shaw to thump in a rising shot that was easily plucked out of the air by big Joe Corrigan in the City goal. Minutes later, Dennis Mortimer fed the ball wide to Withe, who whipped in a low cross that Caton turned behind. When the corner came over Shaw was held by Bennett but, to the crowd's displeasure, the referee waved away Villa's claims for a penalty.

Peter Withe and Gary Shaw were pulling City's defence all over the park, with Booth and Caton resorting to some crude tackles to stop the Villa duo. In Villa's next attack, Mortimer was set up by a combination of Morley and Withe on the left. The skipper bent in a curler that forced a good diving save from Corrigan. Then Gary Shaw swivelled and, all in one movement, scraped the top of the crossbar with a dipping shot. Tommy Booth set City hearts a-flutter when he got it all wrong just outside his own area. The central defender side-footed the ball to Des Bremner, who raced towards goal, and only a great saving tackle by Bobby McDonald prevented the Scot from getting in a shot.

Dennis Mortimer was everywhere, tidying up in defence and midfield, and prompting attacks with each of his runs from deep. From two of his crosses, McNaught and Evans got in powerful headers that flew just wide. Just after the half-hour, City stormed on to the attack. Paul Power redirected Hutchinson's long ball to Gow, who smashed a shot against Evans. That set up a machine-gun effect, with a quick succession of follow-up shots from Reeves and Mackenzie that were blocked by McNaught and Cowans. The sudden change in City's approach was amazing, and they must have considered themselves unlucky not to score. Mackenzie headed over, then Bennett waltzed around Evans into the area, but McNaught's well-timed tackle saved the day. Next, Deacy was left for dead by Hutchinson, but his final pass was too close to Kenny Swain, who booted clear.

In the final minutes of the half, Villa managed to re-establish a little order to their play. Mortimer's penetrating run down the right resulted in a fine cross to Withe, who combined superbly with

---

Aston Villa 1

Shaw (2)

Manchester City 0

ASTON VILLA v. MANCHESTER CITY

Ron Saunders talks to the press after resigning.

Cowans to create a shooting chance for the Villa midfielder, but the right-foot shot was tame and bounced through to Corrigan. Cowans almost made amends with a great run and pass into the middle that Morley couldn't quite reach and the ball ran behind for a goal-kick. Half-time: Villa 1 City 0.

The second half didn't have as many unforced errors, but both defences were kept busy. Allan Evans brought gasps of disbelief from Villa fans when his despairing lunge scythed down Paul Power. Thankfully, the foul was a few inches outside the penalty area. Gerry Gow failed to bend his free-kick round the Villa wall, and Gary Shaw hoofed the ball away. Soon after, Ken McNaught sent Shaw racing clear and, when the youngster's cross rebounded back to him, the young striker miscontrolled the ball and it spun away. Cowans was playing some lovely football, spraying passes all around the park. Now he floated over a slide-rule cross to Corrigan's right-hand post that Peter Withe headed powerfully towards the top corner, but the City 'keeper leaped athletically to catch the ball.

In City's next attack, Paul Power got in the way of Dave Bennett's low shot, and the ball ran towards Rimmer. The Villa 'keeper looked to have safely gathered the ball, but it span out of his hands towards the goal line. Fortunately, he managed to grab the ball before it crept inside the post. Moments later, Shaw fed Morley on the left. The winger cut inside and drilled a fierce shot that bounced behind, off Corrigan's body. On sixty minutes, after Reeves and Bennett had headed over,

Ken McNaught was hurt making a tackle. The trainer bandaged his leg but, in the end, he had to be carried off, needing eight stitches in a gash above his knee. Ron Saunders sent on David Geddis and moved Des Bremner into defence.

When Booth crudely hacked down Peter Withe, the referee reached for his notebook in a bid to end the unsavoury tackling and Booth was booked. Gary Shaw swivelled to meet the resultant free-kick to smash in a right-footer that Corrigan knocked down and grabbed at the second attempt. A few minutes later Morley should have scored but dragged his shot wide with only Corrigan to beat. On seventy-five minutes, Hutchinson had his name taken for a flying tackle that left Morley spread-eagled on the left wing. From then on in, the game deteriorated into a series of awful tackles by City and missed efforts by Villa. Still, winning 1-0 was better than drawing, and kept Villa hot on Ipswich's heels in second place.

Lowly Leicester beat Liverpool 2-1 at Anfield, Ipswich hammered Stoke 4-0, Manchester United beat Birmingham 2-0, Everton and West Bromwich Albion lost and Arsenal drew. In the Second Division, Chelsea entertained Shrewsbury at Stamford Bridge. The Pensioners won 3-0 to go third behind West Ham and Notts County; haven't the fortunes of football changed for these two clubs?

The First Division table:

	PLD	W	D	L	F	A	PTS
Ipswich	27	15	10	2	51	22	40
Aston Villa	**28**	**17**	**6**	**5**	**47**	**24**	**40**
Liverpool	28	12	12	4	48	31	36
Southampton	28	13	7	8	56	40	33
WBA	27	12	9	6	35	26	33
Arsenal	28	12	11	6	41	33	33

Aston Villa: Rimmer, Swain, Deacy, Evans, McNaught (Geddis), Mortimer, Bremner, Shaw, Withe, Cowans, Morley.

Manchester City: Corrigan, Henry, McDonald, Booth, Caton, Power, Bennett, Gow, MacKenzie, Hutchinson, Reeves. Sub: Tueart.

EVERTON v. ASTON VILLA

Football League First Division, Goodison Park
Referee: Mr G.P. Owen (Anglesey)

Date: Saturday 7 February 1981
Attendance: 31,434

Ken McNaught's leg injury had improved sufficiently for him to face his former club. Gary Williams returned at left-back and Eamonn Deacy was named substitute. Everton, who were in free-fall having only taken one point from their last five games, included young midfielder Gary Megson in place of suspended Steve McMahon.

Villa set off at an electric pace and scored a great goal in the third minute. Gary Shaw latched onto a clearance on the left of the halfway line and switched the ball to Tony Morley. The winger raced into the Toffees' penalty area, drew Martin Hodge out of his goal and fired in a crackerjack of a rising drive that flew into the roof of the net. The early goal didn't slow Villa's attacking brio in any way, and they laid siege to Hodge's goal for the next ten minutes, almost extending their lead in the fourteenth minute. Peter Withe headed a floated far-post free-kick down to Gary Shaw, who let fly with a right-foot volley that dipped and swerved, before rebounding clear off the Everton crossbar. Villa came forward again, with Withe touching Cowans' through ball to Kenny Swain. Villa's right-back sidestepped into the penalty area, and drilled a low shot that forced Hodge to dive full-length to his left to deny Villa a second goal.

Just past the half-hour, Everton mounted a serious attack on the right that led to Eastoe unleashing a wicked shot that Rimmer palmed into the air. The ball bounced down to Megson, who spooned a hurried shot high over the bar. In the thirty-fifth minute, Villa were stunned by a penalty decision that gave Everton their equaliser. Mike Lyons lofted the ball into the area where Ken McNaught beat Peter Eastoe to get the ball away. Everton hands shot up claiming a penalty. Initially referee Owen waved play on, but then changed his mind when his linesman indicated that the McNaught had used his hands to control the ball. Penalty! Trevor Ross gave Rimmer no chance from twelve yards.

The Merseysiders were level for only seven minutes. Dennis Mortimer surged forward, chasing a long clearance up the middle and, with Gary Shaw looking to be in an offside position, the Everton defence hesitated. However, the linesman kept his flag down, and the Villa skipper ran on to take the ball around Hodge and slot a simple side-footer into the empty net. Half-time: Everton 1 Villa 2.

Villa began the second period hungry for another goal, while the Merseysiders were still complaining to the referee that Shaw had been at least a yard offside. As far as Villa were concerned, the score was 2-1. Everton did get forward, but when Asa Hartford's shot was scrambled away from the Villa goal line, the ball was hoofed into the Toffees' half, where Withe showed great control to take the ball in his stride. The big striker surged into the area and tried to take the ball round Hodge, who sprinted from his line to dive bravely at Withe's feet to push the ball away.

Just after the hour mark Megson made a good run down the right, slinging the ball into the area for Imre Varadi to send a first-time volley over Rimmer's crossbar. Then Mike Lyons made a hash

Everton 1	Aston Villa 3
Ross (penalty, 35)	Morley (3)
	Mortimer (42)
	Cowans (penalty, 71)

Villa's ace penalty taker Gordon Cowans.

of his clearance, allowing Gary Shaw to whip the ball away before racing into the area, where he wasted the chance by shooting weakly into Hodge's arms.

Villa grabbed a third goal in the seventy-first minute. Gary Shaw chased a hopeful through ball into the penalty area, where Mike Lyons stupidly grabbed hold of his arm to drag the youngster back when the ball looked like it had run away from him. It was a clear penalty, and referee Owen had no hesitation in pointing to the spot. Up stepped penalty king Gordon Cowans to put the ball past Hodge to give Villa a 3-1 lead. Everton never recovered enough composure to threaten the Villa goal seriously, and the visitors accepted the points eagerly. Job done.

Ipswich beat Crystal Palace 3-2 to retain the lead at the top of the table. West Bromwich Albion beat Liverpool 2-0 and Leicester beat Manchester United 1-0. Arsenal drew.

On 10 February, the second legs of the League Cup semi-finals saw Liverpool beat Manchester City and West Ham triumph over Coventry. And, on the other side of the world, in Tokyo's National Stadium on 11 February, Nottingham Forest were beaten 1-0 in the World Club Championship by Nacional of Uruguay. The Football League referees, to a man, protested against the abolition of the red and yellow card system.

Everton v. Aston Villa

Saturday 14 February 1981 was FA Cup fifth round day. Of the top teams in the league, Ipswich beat Charlton Athletic 2-0 and Everton drew 0-0 at Southampton; three days later Everton won the replay 1-0.

The first league match to be played on a Sunday took place on 15 February, when Darlington played Mansfield in a Fourth Division match at their Feethams ground. Sunday football was to continue in the Second, Third and Fourth Divisions for the remainder of the season.

On 17 February, Ipswich won their third game in a row by beating Middlesbrough 1-0 to open up a two-point lead over Villa in the race for the championship. Both teams had now played 29 games.

Gary Williams' sterling performances earned him an England Under-21 call-up, joining teammate Gary Shaw in the squad for the international against Eire at Anfield on Wednesday 25 February 1981.

Everton: Hodge, Ratcliffe, Bailey, Wright, Lyons, Ross, Megson, Eastoe, Varadi, Hartford, O'Keefe (Lodge).

Aston Villa: Rimmer, Swain, Williams, Evans, McNaught, Mortimer, Bremner, Shaw, Withe, Cowans, Morley. Sub: Deacy.

ASTON VILLA v. CRYSTAL PALACE

Football League First Division, Villa Park

Referee: Mr D. Richardson (Great Harwood)

Date: Saturday 21 February 1981

Attendance: 27,203

A midweek flu virus that had affected a number of players had fortunately cleared up by the weekend. Jimmy Rimmer passed a late fitness test on his injured thigh. Crystal Palace's new manager, Dario Gradi, was less fortunate. Defenders Jim Cannon, Billy Gilbert, Steve Lovell, 'keeper Paul Barron and ex-England captain, midfielder Gerry Francis, were injured or suspended. Striker Ian Walsh was dropped. England Under-21 defender Terry Fenwick had been sold to QPR in December for £100,000, along with striker Mike Flanagan, who cost QPR £150,000. Little wonder that Palace were rooted to the bottom of the First Division. At centre forward, Palace had nineteen-year-old Clive Allen. Allen had scored 32 goals in 49 games for QPR, and joined Arsenal in June 1980 in a deal worth £1.25 million. Then, two months later, in one of football's most bizarre transfers, he'd been transferred to Palace for around £800,000 without having kicked a ball for Arsenal.

In the fourth minute, Villa hit Palace with a body blow. Tony Morley smacked in a thunderbolt that 'keeper David Fry did well to palm away. The ball reached Gary Shaw, who switched it back to Morley, and Morley's centre was headed home by Peter Withe for his twelfth goal of the season in all competitions. Three minutes later, Villa went close to a second from a Cowans' corner, but the Palace defence managed to shut the door on McNaught and Withe before they could shoot. In the ninth minute, Des Bremner nodded on to Withe, who laid a clever pass to Cowans. The midfielder unleashed a tremendous rising shot, but Fry was perfectly positioned to claim the ball. Palace were presented with an opportunity when Rimmer's poorly struck goal-kick was pulled down by Neil Smillie, who hit the top of the bar with a speculative effort from twenty-five yards. Villa hit back with a corner, which Cowans sent to the far post. Bremner nodded it into the six-yard box, where Peter Withe chest-trapped the ball and in one movement swivelled to crash in a shot that flashed wide of Fry's post.

Villa's play had become more ragged, allowing Palace to intercept a number of half-hearted and misdirected passes, much to the annoyance of the home supporters. But then Morley waltzed round Paul Hinshelwood before whipping his cross to the near-post for Shaw to flick a header that went behind off a defender. Referee Richardson gave a goal-kick, to the derision of the Villa fans. Fry was called into action a few minutes later to smother a twenty-five-yard snap-shot from Withe, after McNaught's cross had been knocked down to him. Five minutes before the break, Mortimer lobbed a great cross over the defenders to set up Withe, whose tame first-timer bounced past the far post. One minute before the interval, a surging Morley run warmed up the crowd, but the winger's angled shot hit the side-netting. In the last action of the half, Mortimer volleyed a right-wing throw-in the wrong side of the post. Half-time: Villa 1 Palace 0.

Aston Villa 2	Crystal Palace 1
Withe 2 (4 & 70)	Hinshelwood (71)

ASTON VILLA v. CRYSTAL PALACE

Peter Withe.

Palace began the second period with a swift move that led to Shaun Brooks setting up a half-chance for Vince Hilaire that had Rimmer scrambling from his line to smother the ball. In the forty-ninth minute, there was bad news for Villa when Gary Williams pulled a leg muscle, and was forced to limp off to be replaced by Colin Gibson. Then Palace's twenty-one-year-old 'keeper leapt athletically to punch out Gibson's floated centre, but the ball fell to Bremner, who swung it back into the box. Gary Shaw turned to fire in a rising shot that Fry kept out with an amazing piece of agility, twisting his body in mid-air to keep the deficit to one goal. After Tony Morley had squared up to Welshman Peter Nicholas following a robust challenge, the referee gave them a dressing down and made them shake hands. Nicholas retaliated with a fierce twenty-yard shot that took a wicked deflection, and Rimmer was thankful to grab the ball as it bounced awkwardly, after a piece of sloppy play from Gibson had let in the midfielder.

The game had taken on a boring look, with neither side putting their heart and soul into it. The crowd needed a lift, and finally got it when Peter Withe sent Morley racing clear with a fantastic overhead kick. The precocious winger zigzagged through the Palace defence but finished with a shot that Fry watched soar across the box and out of play. David Fry was having a great game, and impressed again in the sixty-eighth minute. Withe sprinted into the box to crash a left-foot shot that rebounded clear off the 'keeper's hands. Two minutes later, the Palace 'keeper was wrong-footed by his own centre half. Gordon Cowans swung in a dangerous free-kick that Terry Boyle inadvertently headed back across his own box. In the goalmouth melée, Peter Withe poked the ball over the line for his second goal of the game.

Villa knew they had the game wrapped up, and didn't appear to be concerned when referee Richardson overruled his linesman to award Palace a free-kick on the edge of the Villa penalty area. Twenty-one-year-old Vince Hilaire bent the ball round the Villa wall with the outside of his boot and, with Rimmer hesitating, Paul Hinshelwood raced in at the near post to prod the ball home. From then on in, Villa drew bodies behind the ball, intent on hanging on for both points. Palace seemed to be content just to have scored a goal against Villa, and rather left it at that.

Ipswich beat Wolves 3-1 and Liverpool drew 2-2 at Brighton. Arsenal and Manchester United both lost.

The First Division table:

	PLD	W	D	L	F	A	PTS
Ipswich Town	30	18	10	2	58	25	46
Aston Villa	**30**	**19**	**6**	**5**	**52**	**26**	**44**
Liverpool	31	12	14	5	52	37	38
WBA	30	14	10	6	41	28	38
Southampton	30	14	8	8	60	43	36
Nottm Forest	30	14	8	8	47	32	36

On Wednesday 25 February at Anfield the England Under-21s beat Eire 1-0 with a Gary Shaw goal.

Aston Villa: Rimmer, Swain, Williams (Gibson), Evans, McNaught, Mortimer, Bremner, Shaw, Withe, Cowans, Morley.

Crystal Palace: Fry, Hinshelwood, Dare, Nicholas, Boyle, Banfield, Smillie, Brooks, Allen, Sealy, Hilaire. Sub: Leahy.

WOLVERHAMPTON WANDERERS v. ASTON VILLA

Football League First Division, Molineux
Referee: Mr Joe Worrall (Warrington)

Date: Saturday 28 February 1981
Attendance: 34,693

Villa were unchanged, with Gary Williams' pulled muscle improving sufficiently for him to resume at left-back. Wolves had Willie Carr back after missing five games through injury. Strikers Peter Withe and Andy Gray both faced former clubs.

The atmosphere inside Molineux was electric. Villa swept upfield from the kick-off, but the ball was given away and Wolves broke forward with a long ball to Andy Gray just outside the penalty area. The ex-Villa favourite crashed in a shot that rebounded off Williams to Peter Daniel, who tried a curler that Jimmy Rimmer caught comfortably. Then Evans shoved Gray to give away a free-kick that Hibbitt curled into the box, but Rimmer gathered under Gray's challenge. Wolves were applying plenty of pressure on the Villa backline with Richards and Gray chasing every cross and through ball. On the left flank, Mel Eves was giving Swain plenty to think about. Finally, Villa managed to escape Wolves' stranglehold. Gary Shaw touched a through ball towards the area for Des Bremner to race onto, but as the midfielder was about to pull the trigger Derek Parkin stretched to deflect the ball for a corner. George Berry was rather fortunate not to be booked when he scythed down Kenny Swain. Gordon Cowans flighted a poor ball into the box, where Paul Bradshaw made an easy catch.

All hell broke loose in the eighteenth minute when Tony Morley made a dangerous two-footed tackle on Peter Daniel. Andy Gray was incensed, but before the incident deteriorated into fisticuffs, referee Joe Worrall stepped in to calm things down, delivering a good telling off. Amazingly, Morley wasn't booked. Daniel resumed after the magic sponge had been applied but, a few minutes later, was forced to limp off. Norman Bell came on to lead Wolves' attack, with John Richards moving to midfield. On twenty-five minutes, Swain hit a crossfield pass to free Morley on the left. The winger cut inside to unleash a low shot that beat the diving Bradshaw but flashed just wide of the far post.

A few minutes later, players and crowd alike were stopped in their tracks. An ambulance drove along the Molineux Street Stand touchline, picked up Peter Daniel and whisked him off to hospital for examination. When play resumed, Carr went close with a header from Hibbitt's corner-kick. Villa countered when Cowans sent Morley away on the left with a beautiful crossfield pass. The left winger accelerated along the touchline before swinging in a near-post cross. Gary Shaw nipped in to flick the ball goalwards, but Bradshaw managed to knock it out for a corner on the left. The short corner was whipped into the box and headed out to Dennis Mortimer, whose rasping shot scraped the top of Bradshaw's crossbar. In injury time, Villa had a great chance to score. The move started in the centre circle when Withe skilfully chested the ball to Mortimer, who found Morley in space. The winger raced into the box but, with only Bradshaw to beat, he shot tamely into the 'keeper's arms. Half-time: 0-0.

Wolverhampton Wanderers 0

Aston Villa 1
Withe (83)

WOLVERHAMPTON WANDERERS v. ASTON VILLA

Gary Williams.

After Eves had headed out Morley's near-post corner-kick, Mortimer latched onto the ball, but dragged his first-time screamer well wide. Six minutes after the restart, Wolves put together a fine move that ended with a left-wing cross from Norman Bell. The far-post ball was controlled beautifully by the unmarked Andy Gray. The striker turned sharply to fire in a low shot that rebounded off Rimmer's leg to Richards, who nudged it home. The Wolves fans went crackers with delight, but referee Joe Worrall halted the celebrations, with an offside decision that brought a chorus of boos and jeers from the terraces.

The game was turning into a bit of a bad tempered affair, fuelled by a few tasty tackles from both sides. Morley was still being singled out by the crowd for his bone-crunching challenge on Daniel. There seemed to be more than a little afters involved when Andy Gray launched himself into Tony Morley, leaving the winger spread-eagled on the ground. Dennis Mortimer exchanged a few choice words with Gray, until the referee parted them. On fifty-five minutes the Villa skipper latched onto a loose ball to crack in a first-timer that Bradshaw kept out brilliantly, diving low to his right. At the other end, Rimmer made an instinctive save to prevent Richards getting his name on the scoresheet. Then Bradshaw dived low to stop a Cowans thunderbolt. For the next twenty-five minutes, the game ebbed and flowed with neither side managing to trouble the goalkeepers seriously. Then, in an exciting final eight minutes, chances came thick and fast. In the eighty-second minute Andy Gray was guilty of a glaring miss. Then, with seven minutes remaining, Villa won a corner on the left. Tony Morley swung the ball into the box and Peter Withe rose highest to head Allan Evans' flick on past Bradshaw. And that, as they say, was that. Andy Gray's miss had dire consequences for Wolves, and gave Villa a double over their West Midlands rivals.

WOLVERHAMPTON WANDERERS *v.* ASTON VILLA

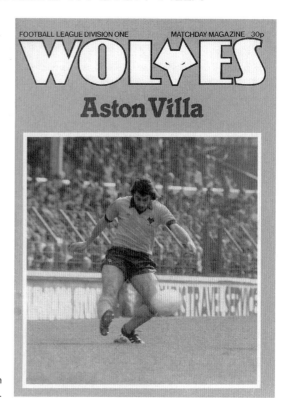

The programme from the game Wolverhampton
Wanderers *v.* Aston Villa. 28 February 1981.

Villa stayed second because Ipswich walloped Coventry 4-0 at Highfield Road. Liverpool beat Southampton 2-0, Everton won 3-2 at Crystal Palace, Arsenal and West Bromwich Albion drew, and Manchester United lost.

Villa had another chance to catch up a little on Ipswich on the following Saturday. The Suffolk boys were due to play Nottingham Forest in the sixth round of the FA Cup, having thumped St Etienne 4-1 in France on Wednesday 4 March in the first leg of their UEFA Cup quarter-final.

Wolverhampton Wanderers: Bradshaw, Palmer, Parkin, Daniel (Bell), McAlle, Berry, Hibbitt, Carr, Gray, Richards, Eves.

Aston Villa: Rimmer, Swain, Williams, Evans, McNaught, Mortimer, Bremner, Shaw, Withe, Cowans, Morley. Sub: Gibson

SUNDERLAND v. ASTON VILLA

Football League First Division, Roker Park
Referee: Mr C.N. Seel (Carlisle)

Date: Saturday 7 March 1981
Attendance: 27,278

Ron Saunders was off with flu, but that didn't reduce unchanged Villa's effectiveness in any way. They almost went ahead after only thirty seconds. Kenny Swain intercepted Gordon Chisholm's misplaced ball out of defence and swept upfield, before smashing a twenty-five-yarder inches wide. Less than a minute later Villa took the lead with a superb move that oozed class. Peter Withe laid the ball back to Tony Morley who whipped in a far-post cross that Allan Evans powered bullet-like with his head past 'keeper Barry Siddall.

Minutes later, a short corner by Gordon Cowans was fed to the near post. Gary Shaw turned the ball the wrong side of Siddall's post. On eighteen minutes, Peter Withe found the ball at his feet when a cross bounced to him, but although he turned adroitly, his low shot fractionally missed the far post. However, when Withe went enthusiastically into his next challenge, referee Seel delivered a stern lecture for over-exuberance.

One minute later Villa went further ahead. Dennis Mortimer took a fabulous defence-splitting pass from Cowans before setting off on an incisive trademark sprint from midfield, to beat Siddall's despairing dive with a perfect left-foot drive that curved inside the far post.

In the twenty-third minute Kenny Swain intercepted a through ball, then was on the receiving end of a firm challenge from Tom Ritchie. Referee Seel gave a free-kick against the Villa full-back who was adjudged to have upended the Sunderland striker. Swain wasn't happy, and earned a booking for dissent. Villa won a corner in the thirty-third minute. Morley fired the flag-kick into the box, where Ken McNaught's first-time lunge was punched clear by Siddall. With the clock ticking away to half-time, Sunderland swept onto the attack, but Des Bremner got across well to jockey away the danger. However, the referee penalised the Villa midfielder for obstruction. Arnott curled the ball to the near post, where the inrushing Ritchie planted a firm header straight at Rimmer. Half-time: Sunderland 0 Villa 2.

Sunderland brought on striker John Cooke to replace the injured Bowyer for the start of the second half, and immediately won a corner. Stan Cummins lobbed the ball into the box, where Rimmer dived bravely to smother the ball at the second attempt. With the famous 'Roker Roar' ringing in their ears, Sunderland flew at Villa. A crunching touchline challenge, in the fifty-third minute, left Ken McNaught and Joe Hinnigan needing treatment before they could return to the action. In the fifty-seventh minute Peter Withe headed McNaught's long free-kick towards goal, but Siddall got down smartly to clutch the ball on the line. Back came Sunderland with an attack that almost brought a goal. Ken McNaught tried to play the ball back to Rimmer, but Stan Cummins was onto it in a flash. But, after rounding Rimmer, the diminutive midfielder's shot bounced behind off the outside of the post.

Sunderland 1	Aston Villa 2
Hinnigan (68)	Evans (2)
	Mortimer (19)

117

SUNDERLAND *v.* ASTON VILLA

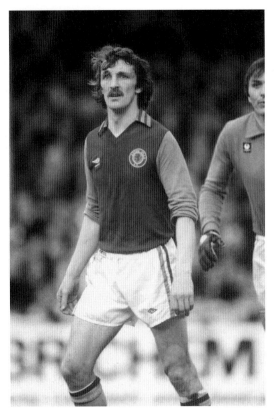

Des Bremner

Gary Rowell earned a deserved booking for tripping Tony Morley from behind. Minutes later, Stan Cummins latched onto a neat pass from Arnott. Fortunately, Jimmy Rimmer was able to knock down his left-foot shot before diving to smother the ball. Villa hit back with a lightning attack that led to Mortimer jabbing the ball to Gary Shaw, who sped past Hindmarch, only to have his legs whipped from under him from behind. Amazingly Hindmarch escaped with just a free-kick against him. Then in the sixty-eighth minute, Sunderland pulled a goal back to set up a frenetic final twenty minutes. Stan Cummins was floored just outside the Villa penalty area and, when Kevin Arnott floated the free-kick to the far post, Joe Hinnigan nipped in between Rimmer and Evans to power a header into the net. Roker Park erupted with glee.

In the seventy-third minute, Peter Withe was booked for complaining after the referee had awarded the Wearsiders a free-kick. Then in the final minutes, Villa's number nine missed an absolute sitter, when he should have put the game beyond Sunderland's reach.

Ipswich drew 3-3 at Nottingham Forest to stay on top of the division. Villa remained second. In the FA Cup sixth round, Everton drew 2-2 with Manchester City.

On the following Tuesday evening, 10 March, Dutch ace Arnold Muhren kept Ipswich on course for a history-making treble when he scored a sixty-seventh-minute winner in a pulsating FA Cup sixth round replay to beat Nottingham Forest 1-0 at Portman Road. In the other replay, Wolves disposed of Middlesbrough 3-1 after extra time, courtesy of goals by Mel Eves, John Richards and

Norman Bell. Joining them in the semi-finals were Spurs and Manchester City. Also on 10 March, Aston Villa announced that assistant commercial manager Sue Walker, aged thirty-three, had been appointed commercial manager at Villa Park, beating twenty-nine other applicants to the job. She became the first woman to hold such a post, reputedly saying: 'It is a great breakthrough for a female in what has always been regarded as a man's world. But I do not see any problems.'

Bolton, Newcastle and Nottingham Forest were each fined the minimum £1,000 by the FA for displaying their sponsors' name on their shirts during FA Cup matches. Forest were already appealing against a fine of £7,000 imposed by UEFA in February for shirt advertising during their European Super Cup tie with Valencia.

First Division Table:

	PLD	W	D	L	F	A	PTS
Ipswich	31	19	10	2	62	25	48
Aston Villa	**32**	**21**	**6**	**5**	**55**	**27**	**48**
WBA	32	15	11	6	44	30	41
Liverpool	33	13	14	5	54	37	40
Nottm Forest	32	15	9	8	49	33	39
Southampton	33	15	8	10	61	47	38

On the home front, Chancellor Geoffrey Howe's budget smacked smokers, drinkers and motorists for six. Cigarettes went up 14p a packet of twenty; 4p went on a pint of beer, 12p on a bottle of wine and 60p on a bottle of spirits. Petrol rose by 20p a gallon, and road tax increased by £10 to £70.

Sunderland: Siddall, Hinnigan, Bolton, Hindmarch, Elliott, Rowell, Arnott, Bowyer (Cooke), Ritchie, Chisholm, Cummins.

Aston Villa: Rimmer, Swain, Williams, Evans, McNaught (Gibson), Mortimer, Bremner, Shaw, Withe, Cowans, Morley.

ASTON VILLA v. MANCHESTER UNITED

Football League First Division, Villa Park

Referee: Mr D.V. Reeves (Uxbridge)

Date: Saturday 14 March 1981

Attendance: 42,182

In midweek, Jimmy Rimmer had been rushed to hospital with a nasty cut on his eyebrow, the result of a training ground collision with Allan Evans. Dave Sexton's United were also unchanged, despite not scoring in the previous five league games, losing the last three 1-0. It had rained heavily in the days preceding this match, so it was with tremendous pride that the Villa groundstaff removed the protective covering to reveal a reasonably dry playing surface.

From the kick-off, Bremner combined well with Shaw to win a throw-in that was laid off to Mortimer, who drilled in a low shot that 'keeper Gary Bailey dived to smother. Then, after Withe and Shaw had tried to break through, Cowans was pushed over by Macari to win a free-kick. Mortimer touched the ball to Cowans, who unleashed a tremendous low shot that flashed past the post. In the ninth minute, Tony Morley went close, latching onto Withe's headed flick, before swerving inside Jimmy Nicholl, to rifle in a low shot. Bailey dived to his left to push the ball away, but before it could cross the line, it was booted clear. Then Lou Macari spotted Rimmer off his line and fired in a first-time lob that flew over the Villa 'keeper's head onto the roof of the net. In the sixteenth minute, Villa took the lead with a classic goal from Peter Withe. Gordon Cowans slipped the ball down the right, where Kenny Swain left Arthur Albiston for dead, before swinging over an inch-perfect cross for Withe to head home. For the next few minutes it was nip and tuck as both sides looked for a goal.

On twenty-five minutes it looked like Villa would grab a second. Swain overlapped on the right and crossed the ball into the box. Gary Shaw found himself unmarked as the ball dropped to him, but with only Bailey to beat, the youngster rushed his shot and the ball drifted wide of the target. Fortunately, Villa had only three minutes to wait before they scored again. A short corner on the left by Cowans was hooked to the far post by Morley, where Joe Jordan mistimed his header and nodded the ball back into his own area. The ball dropped to Peter Withe, whose first-time shot bounced away off a defender. Villa's centre forward raced after it, and placed a marvellous shot on the turn beyond Bailey into the corner of the net. Then Cowans got into a good position when Withe turned provider with a neat cross from the right, but he allowed the ball to bounce and the chance was gone. Half-time: Villa 2 Manchester United 0.

Maybe Villa were a little over-confident at the start of the second-period, allowing United time and space to come at them. Coppell threatened on the right, catching Villa's defence unawares by chipping the ball to the far post, where Macari forced Rimmer to make a fabulous leaping save. However, the ball dropped to Joe Jordan's head, who made no mistake from six yards to bring United a glimmer of hope.

For the next ten minutes, Villa went to pieces and, when Sammy McIlroy fired low across the goalmouth, Rimmer had to be quick to stop Macari's diving header on the line. However, Villa

Aston Villa 3	Manchester United 3
Withe 2 (16 & 28)	Jordan 2 (46 & 66)
Shaw (68)	McIllroy (penalty, 88)

Peter Withe
in action.

weren't done, and hit back with a first-time piledriver from Gordon Cowans that had Gary Bailey stretching full-length to make a fantastic diving save. In the sixty-sixth minute Joe Jordan darted in to power home Coppell's right-wing cross to make it 2-2. The United fans went crazy with joy, but two minutes later, their cheers turned to tears, as Villa regained the lead in this topsy-turvy game. Gary Shaw latched onto the ball and drilled an inch-perfect shot just inside Bailey's post. Time for Villa to batten down the hatches as United threw everything at them. In the eighty-eighth minute, after a number of close calls, Villa conceded a penalty when Gary Williams felled Steve Coppell in the area. Up stepped Sammy McIlroy to send the ball past Rimmer to bring the scores level again. The second 3-3 draw with the Red Devils in one season – amazing!

Ipswich beat Spurs 3-0, their sixth successive league victory in an unbeaten run of twelve games.

The First Division table:

	PLD	W	D	L	F	A	PTS
Ipswich Town	32	20	10	2	65	25	50
Aston Villa	**33**	**21**	**7**	**5**	**58**	**30**	**49**
Nottm Forest	33	16	9	8	53	34	41
WBA	33	15	11	7	45	32	41
Liverpool	32	13	14	5	54	37	40

In the League Cup final at Wembley on 15 March, Liverpool and West Ham drew 1-1. Three days later at Portman Road, Ipswich beat St Etienne 3-1 in the second leg of their UEFA Cup quarter-final to win the tie 7-2.

Aston Villa: Rimmer, Swain, Williams, Evans, McNaught, Mortimer, Bremner, Shaw, Withe, Cowans, Morley.
   Sub: Gibson.
Manchester United: Bailey, Nicholl, Albiston, Wilkins, Moran, Buchan, Coppell, Birtles, Jordan, Macari, McIlroy.
   Sub: Duxbury.

TOTTENHAM HOTSPUR v. ASTON VILLA

Football League First Division, White Hart Lane   **Date:** Saturday 21 March 1981
Referee: Mr L.F. Burden (Corfe Mullen, Dorset)   **Attendance:** 35,091

Peter Withe started a two-match suspension, so Ron Saunders brought in David Geddis. Tottenham manager Keith Burkinshaw brought in Staffordshire-born goalkeeper Milija Aleksic for only his fourth start of the season in place of the injured Barry Daines.

In the first minute, Spurs attacked down the left wing. Gary Brooke whipped in a vicious low cross that Jimmy Rimmer failed to reach with a despairing dive. Luckily, the ball ran out of play on the opposite touchline. In Villa's first attack Gary Shaw sped into the left of the area, before chipping the ball to the far post, where Paul Miller beat David Geddis to the ball to head over his own bar. Then Gary Williams hit a delightful ball along the left touchline for Tony Morley, who whipped a low near-post centre into the box. Paul Miller swung a boot to clear. The ball looped into the air, the swirling wind carrying the ball towards goal, forcing Aleksic to palm it over the bar. The gusting, blustery weather was certainly creating a few problems. Another surge forward by Villa took Des Bremner to the edge of the penalty area, but his weak shot was easily gathered by Aleksic. Then Shaw went close with a curling shot on the turn that flashed narrowly wide.

The police were in action to sort out a few minor scuffles after a number of Villa fans had found themselves shepherded into a section of the terraces occupied by Tottenham supporters.

Suddenly Spurs came to life. Steve Archibald's shot from Ossie Ardiles' low cross rebounded kindly for Garth Crooks to smash in a swerving first-timer that Rimmer saved with a superb dive. Villa regained the initiative and, when Gordon Cowans found Dennis Mortimer on the edge of the area it looked odds-on a goal. Unfortunately, the skipper curled his effort well wide. Then disaster struck for Villa when, against the run of play, Spurs grabbed a forty-first minute goal. Chris Hughton overlapped on the left before swinging in a low cross to Gary Brooke. The twenty-year-old from Bethnal Green flicked the ball across the box for Garth Crooks to smash past Rimmer from a tight angle. Villa's shouts for offside fell on deaf ears as referee Burden gave the goal after checking with his linesman – Villa couldn't believe it. Spurs played out the remaining four minutes on the attack, and Brooke forced a diving save from Rimmer, who knocked the ball down for Evans to boot clear. Half-time: Spurs 1 Villa 0.

At the start of the second half, Gary Shaw reacted quickest, collecting a hopeful through ball on the right, before cutting in to drill in a low shot that Aleksic gathered. Then after a Spurs attack had been repulsed, Villa had a great chance to draw level in the fiftieth minute. Shaw turned provider with a lovely pass to David Geddis in the Spurs penalty area, but the striker somehow contrived to scoop his shot over Aleksic's crossbar. The crowd held their breath in the fifty-fourth minute, when the superb Glenn Hoddle let fly with one of his sizzling trademark long-range specials that Rimmer reached, with an athletic spring across his line, to tip the ball over the bar.

Totenham Hotspur 2	Aston Villa 0
Crooks (41)	
Archibald (73)	

TOTTENHAM HOTSPUR v. ASTON VILLA

Gordon Cowans and Tottenham's Ricky Villa in the 1981 Charity Shield game.

Spurs were now besting Villa in many areas of the pitch. Then the spark to ignite a cohesive fightback came out of the blue in the form of a disputed sixty-third-minute penalty. In an innocuous incident, Gary Shaw went over under Graham Roberts' challenge from behind. The referee blew and pointed to the penalty spot. However, the flame of recovery sparked only briefly because Gordon Cowans missed the chance to equalise. Ten minutes later Spurs made sure with a goal that had more than an element of luck attached to it. A couple of speculative shots bounced off Swain and Evans to Tony Galvin, who raced clear on the left wing before floating a perfect centre to the far post, where Steve Archibald out-jumped the Villa defence to power a firm header just inside Rimmer's post.

Villa tried to regroup, but really it was too late. Spurs might even have increased their lead with a couple of late flurries; it wasn't Villa's day. Maybe it would have been if Cowans had tucked away the penalty? Who knows? Fortunately Villa lost no ground on the leaders because Manchester United beat Ipswich 2-1 at Old Trafford. Liverpool beat Scouse rivals Everton 1-0. West Brom beat Forest 2-1 to jump over them into fourth. Southampton had sneaked back up on the rails, with four wins on the trot, to move into third place.

TOTTENHAM HOTSPUR v. ASTON VILLA

The First Division table:

	PLD	W	D	L	F	A	PTS
Ipswich Town	33	20	10	3	66	27	50
Aston Villa	**34**	**21**	**7**	**6**	**58**	**32**	**49**
Southampton	36	18	8	10	67	48	44
WBA	34	16	11	7	47	33	43
Nottm Forest	35	16	10	9	55	37	42
Liverpool	33	14	14	5	55	37	42

On Sunday 22 March British race ace Mike Hailwood sadly died, after fighting for his life in the intensive-care unit of a Birmingham hospital. The forty-year-old's Rover had careered out of control into the back of a lorry. His nine-year-old daughter, Michelle, was also killed; his six-year-old son escaped with cuts and bruises. Apparently the family were on a trip to the chip shop. His wife Pauline was at his bedside.

On 25 March Tony Morley played for England 'B' in a 3-2 defeat by Spain in Granada.

Tottenham Hotspur: Aleksic, Hughton, Miller, Roberts, Brooke, Perryman, Ardiles, Archibald, Galvin, Hoddle, Crooks. Sub: Mazzon.

Aston Villa: Rimmer, Swain, Williams, Evans, McNaught, Mortimer, Bremner, Shaw, Geddis, Cowans, Morley. Sub: Gibson.

ASTON VILLA v. SOUTHAMPTON

Football League First Division, Villa Park
Referee: Mr N.H. Glover (Chorley)

Date: Saturday 28 March 1981
Attendance: 32,467

There was still no Peter Withe to help Villa steady the ship after the defeat at Spurs. Things didn't start too well against the Saints. Despite the close attentions of Kevin Keegan, Allan Evans didn't appear to be under too much pressure when he attempted to get Steve Williams' right-wing cross back to Jimmy Rimmer. However, the centre-back hit his lob too hard, and the ball flew over the Villa 'keeper into the corner of the net.

Villa stormed back and within a minute almost equalised. Dennis Mortimer's snap-shot from the edge of the penalty area had Saints 'keeper Peter Wells groping thin air as the ball flew just wide of the right-hand post. A minute later Cowans burst into the box before hitting a scorching drive that flashed past Wells' left-hand upright. In the eighteenth minute, Kevin Keegan cut inside Gary Williams, before slipping a neat pass to Channon, whose first-time drive was pushed behind by Rimmer. When the corner flew into the area, Gary Williams hooked the ball clear before Channon could reach it.

Saints had definitely silenced the Villa fans with their emphatic play, but then suddenly a huge cheer echoed around Villa Park as the news that Sunderland had taken the lead at Ipswich was flashed onto the scoreboard. Just prior to the half-hour mark, Dennis Mortimer cut in from the left wing, to smash a blistering right-foot drive that beat Wells but smacked against the post before bouncing clear. A couple of minutes later, Allan Evans almost committed a double sin with a second own goal when he sliced across the ball attempting to clear Ivan Golac's dipping cross, after the Yugoslavian full-back had taken the ball away from Cowans. The ball bounced off Rimmer to Alan Ball, and luckily the World Cup winner skied his shot way over the top. In the thirty-fifth minute Mortimer played the ball back to Morley, who swerved towards goal, only to curl his shot into the side-netting from a tight angle.

So far, Geddis and Shaw hadn't been able to get into the game, and Villa's attacking was mainly left to Mortimer and Morley, but all that changed in the forty-third minute. Geddis brilliantly flicked on Cowans' clearance to Tony Morley, who raced to the penalty area from the halfway line, before smashing the ball beyond Wells' despairing dive to bring Villa back to level terms. Southampton claimed that the winger had been offside, but the referee waved away their protests. Then to complete the turnround, Villa grabbed a second goal. Gary Williams thumped a long ball up to David Geddis, who raced on to blast the ball past Saints' helpless 'keeper to put Villa ahead. Half-time: Villa 2 Southampton 1.

After McNaught had been penalised for pushing Wells at the start of the second period, Gary Williams' ankle was on the receiving end of a nasty kick that needed attention. When the free-kick came in to Saints' box, Gary Shaw tried a first-time shot that sliced away for a goal-kick.

Aston Villa 2	Southampton 1
Morley (43)	Evans (own goal, 11)
Geddis (45)	

Aston Villa v. Southampton

David Geddis scores Villa's winner, watched by Nick Holmes.

Jimmy Rimmer hadn't had much to do, but twelve minutes after the break, he was twice called upon to maintain Villa's lead. First the Villa 'keeper had to sprint from his line to deny Keegan after Steve Moran had headed Graham Baker's centre down in the box. Then Rimmer's bravery was rewarded when he dived at Baker's feet. The ball bounced from the 'keeper's grasp to roll invitingly along the six-yard line, but finally Ken McNaught raced in to boot clear. In the sixty-fifth minute, after a period of indifferent play, Villa began to get their act back together. However, before they could make their renewed flair pay dividends, David Geddis needed lengthy treatment to his right thigh that required heavy bandaging. Almost immediately, Alan Ball went down under a challenge. He too needed lengthy treatment before having to limp from the field in the seventy-first minute to be replaced by David Puckett. The referee's patience had reached its limit, and Allan Evans was booked for a heavy tackle on Mick Channon. Then, with less than ten minutes to go, Dennis Mortimer was the recipient of some wretched luck. He found space on the corner of the Southampton penalty area, only to see his scorching drive bounce to safety off the inside of the far post. The woodwork had denied the Villa skipper twice, but still, Villa took the points, and were back in business.

Arsenal beat Liverpool 1-0 to end virtually the Scousers' dream of a treble. Forest leapfrogged Southampton and West Bromwich Albion with a 2-1 victory over Norwich. Ipswich were fighting hard, beating Sunderland 4-1, to hold onto their one-point advantage over Villa with a game in hand.

Aston Villa v. Southampton

The First Division table:

	PLD	W	D	L	F	A	PTS
Ipswich Town	34	21	10	3	70	28	52
Aston Villa	**35**	**22**	**7**	**6**	**60**	**33**	**51**
Nottm Forest	36	17	10	9	57	38	44
Southampton	37	18	8	11	68	50	44
WBA	35	16	11	8	48	35	43
Liverpool	34	14	14	6	55	38	42

On April Fools' Day, Liverpool won the League Cup, beating West Ham United 2-1 in a replay at Villa Park.

Aston Villa: Rimmer, Swain, Williams, Evans, McNaught, Mortimer, Bremner, Shaw, Geddis, Cowans, Morley. Sub: Deacy.
Southampton: Wells, Golac, Holmes, Williams, Watson, Nicholl, Keegan, Channon, Baker G., Moran, Ball (Puckett).

LEICESTER CITY v. ASTON VILLA

Football League First Division, Filbert Street   **Date:** Saturday 4 April 1981
Referee: Mr T.L. Morris (Leeds)   **Attendance:** 26,032

Peter Withe returned to the starting line-up after completing a two-match suspension, with David Geddis dropping down to the substitute's bench. Other than this Villa were unchanged. Foxes manager Jock Wallace recalled Birmingham-born Geoff Scott at number six in what was a young Leicester team.

Villa went for the jugular from the start. Peter Withe stormed through the middle, knocking Scott out of his way as he went, and drilled in a low shot that Mark Wallington dived to save. However, it wouldn't have counted, because referee Morris had blown for a foul. Jimmy Rimmer was called into action in the eighth minute, sprinting out of his goal to stop an angled drive from Steve Lynex, Leicester's recent £100,000 capture from Birmingham City. Then Dennis Mortimer needed to sprint to his defence's aid to put the ball out, before Jim Melrose could react. On fifteen minutes, Villa were a goal down. A fine pass sent striker Alan Young racing into the left of the Villa penalty area, where he was on the end of a barging challenge by Ken McNaught. The centre forward went down in a heap and the referee pointed to the spot. Steve Lynex gave Rimmer no chance with a firm and accurate shot to give Leicester the lead. After an impressive fifteen minutes packed with determination and an unstinting work-rate, the young Foxes just about deserved it.

Villa were certainly stunned by Leicester's approach and, with the Foxes harrying and chasing, there was little time for midfield creativity. It was Villa's defenders who provided the missing punch. The exemplary Allan Evans got forward to draw a good save from Wallington with a powerful header, before ballooning McNaught's through ball over the top in his next race upfield. In the twentieth minute Melrose was booked for a high tackle when his foot caught Swain. Then, in the twenty-fourth minute, it all came right for Villa. Right-back Tommy Williams brought down Gary Shaw, and Gordon Cowans floated the free-kick into the area. Peter Withe rose like a salmon to direct a perfectly placed glancing header wide of Mark Wallington for the equaliser.

On thirty-three minutes Kenny Swain flew down the right, feeding Gary Shaw, who swerved towards the area to power a blistering cross-shot past Wallington. The ball might have gone wide had Des Bremner not raced in to steer the ball home to give Villa the lead.

Villa had weathered the storm and now took control with some delightful one-touch passing. They almost scored a third in the forty-second minute when Mortimer's right-wing corner reached Evans at the near post. The Scot flick-headed the ball across the box, where Shaw rifled in a fearsome shot that Wallington instinctively palmed down and Paul Friar booted it off the line. Then, a minute before half-time, Rimmer waited for Cowans to push a bouncing high clearance back to him. But as the Villa midfielder waited for the ball to come down, Lynex rushed in between them to whip the ball away and into the net for the equaliser. What a daft goal to give away! Half-time: 2-2.

Leicester City 2   **Aston Villa 4**
  Lynex 2 (penalty, 15 & 44)   Withe 2 (24 & 49)
        Bremner (33)
        Morley (55)

Des Bremner.

Ron Saunders must have delivered a right-royal rollicking during the break, because Villa flew out of the blocks at the start of the second half. When Kenny Swain's forty-ninth-minute right-wing cross came in, Peter Withe repeated his earlier magnificent leap above the Leicester defence to power his header beyond Wallington for his sixteenth league goal of the campaign; 3-2 to Villa. This time Villa seemed determined not to allow Leicester any chance of a comeback and, in the fifty-fifth minute, added a fourth goal to cement a hard-fought victory. Leicester conceded a free-kick a couple of yards outside their penalty area that Cowans touched to his right, where Mortimer squared the ball for Tony Morley to crash a scorching right-foot drive beyond Wallington's dive into the far corner. 4-2! This was the first time Villa had notched four goals in an away league game since 11 November 1978, when they beat Wolves 4-0 at Molineux.

Leicester came at Villa with all guns blazing. On sixty-six minutes, Rimmer raced out to gather a loose ball but missed it, allowing Young to square to Jim Melrose, who had a clear sight of goal. Fortunately, the striker delayed his close-range shot a fraction too long and Allan Evans, who had raced back to cover the goal, was perfectly positioned to boot the ball off the line. Leicester were certainly giving Rimmer a torrid time and, a few minutes later, the Villa 'keeper had to dive full-length to make a fabulous one-handed fingertip save to keep out Young's piledriver.

Leicester City v. Aston Villa

This wasn't one of Gary Shaw's best games, in contrast to his strike partner, who had made a marvellous two-goal return to the side. However, with the game moving into the final stages, the young striker showed the crowd a glimpse of his real talent with a skilful turn and shot that drew a marvellous leaping save from Mark Wallington, who stretched to turn the effort over the bar. Then, in almost the last action of the game, winger Neil Grewcock cut inside to drill in a venomous low shot that brought another diving save from Jimmy Rimmer. In the dying seconds Morley broke through the Leicester rearguard to crack in a ferocious shot that Wallington could only parry, but Wilson was on hand to clear the ball off the line.

This fine win leapfrogged Villa over rivals Ipswich, who had lost 3-1 to West Bromwich Albion at The Hawthorns; their third defeat in four games. Had the pressure finally told on the lads from Suffolk? The destination of the First Division title was now in Villa's hands. The bookies had Villa at 8/11 to win the championship, with Ipswich at 4/1. Southampton beat Forest 2-0, and Arsenal won 1-0 at Brighton to stay in contention.

The First Division table:

	PLD	W	D	L	F	A	PTS
Aston Villa	**36**	**23**	**7**	**6**	**64**	**35**	**53**
Ipswich Town	36	21	10	5	71	34	52
WBA	37	18	11	8	53	36	47
Southampton	38	19	8	11	70	50	46
Liverpool	35	15	14	6	58	39	44
Nottm Forest	37	17	10	10	57	40	44

Leicester City: Wallington, Williams, Friar, Byrne, May, Scott, Lynex, Melrose, Young, Wilson, Grewcock.
   Sub: MacDonald.
Aston Villa: Rimmer, Swain, Williams, Evans, McNaught, Mortimer, Bremner, Shaw, Withe, Cowans, Morley.
   Sub: Geddis.

ASTON VILLA v. WEST BROMWICH ALBION

Football League First Division, Villa Park   **Date:** Wednesday 8 April 1981
Referee: Mr L.C. Shapter (Newton Abbot) (rep. Vic Woods) **Attendance:** 47,998

This fixture had originally been scheduled for Saturday 11 April, but with the FA Cup semi-final between Manchester City and Ipswich being played at Villa Park on that day, Villa's crucial sixth derby game of the season was pulled forward to midweek, giving Villa a great opportunity to open up a three-point gap on their rivals for the title. However, with third-placed Albion fighting for a European place next season this wouldn't be a pushover by any means. Ron Saunders gambled by dropping out-of-form Gary Shaw in favour of David Geddis. Full-back Gary Williams had damaged a hamstring, so Colin Gibson returned to the side, with Deacy named substitute.

Traffic jams around Aston and lengthy queues for the turnstiles spelled disappointment for many fans who failed to get into the ground before the game kicked-off; some were still coming in twenty minutes later. The match receipts netted a cool £95,000.

The nervous tension in the almost capacity crowd of 47,998 (only two short of the official capacity), seemed to spill over to the players, with long periods of the game filled with a catalogue of unbelievable errors. Passes frequently went astray, many leading to tense goalmouth situations in which the ball bounced around only to be finally scrambled clear. Slightly more relaxed Albion were presented with a great chance when Gordon Cowans played the most inconceivably misdirected pass imaginable to Cyrille Regis, who must have been amazed to find himself in front of the Villa goal with only Jimmy Rimmer blocking his path to glory. Big Cyrille stalled, allowing the Villa 'keeper time to sprint out of his goal to block the shot when it came. But before Villa could learn their lesson, a minute later Regis was in behind the defence again, but placed his header wide of the post. Whatever Villa were trying to achieve at this point was a mystery to fans and players alike.

David Geddis was struggling to find any cohesive link-up with Peter Withe and, when the former Ipswich striker finally managed a shot, he fired hopelessly wide. Minutes later, Tony Morley dashed round Brendan Batson to fire across an in-swinging ball that inrushing Ken McNaught headed over the Baggies' crossbar. In the forty-fourth minute, Bryan Robson latched onto a loose ball and surged into the Villa penalty area, where only a brave dive at the England midfielder's feet by Jimmy Rimmer prevented a goal, the ball flying high and wide of the danger area. Half-time: 0-0.

Referee Lester Shapter had pulled a leg muscle during the first half, and was replaced in the forty-sixth minute by linesman Vic Wood from Southampton. Gordon Cowans' silky skills seemed to have deserted him. Whenever he got the ball, he failed to find a Villa shirt with his pass. In fact, he was a continual source of half-chances for West Brom, courtesy of his misplaced passes that went everywhere but where they were intended. The euphoria of the opening minutes of the second half soon passed, and the game drifted back into a bit of a non-event that seemed destined for a goal-less draw. Then, on eighty minutes, Tony Morley slalomed his way in and out of John Wile and Alastair

Aston Villa 1	West Bromwich Albion 0
Withe (88)	

ASTON VILLA v. WEST BROMWICH ALBION

Gary Shaw.

Robertson as if they were standing still, before delivering a fabulous pass to Dennis Mortimer, who unleashed a tremendous rising drive that was well held by the diving Tony Godden.

With only a few minutes remaining, Albion took on the look of a team content to take one point from this dour but hard fought game. But, in the eighty-eighth minute, misfortune took a hand to snatch that point away in a single moment of madness. Tony Morley pressured Batson into attempting a needless thirty-yard lob back to his advancing goalkeeper. Peter Withe raced in to intercept the ball and, despite a robust challenge from Ally Robertson, the twenty-nine-year-old Liverpudlian striker calmly lobbed the ball high over the stranded Tony Godden. This was his seventeenth league goal of the season, one better than his previous best, when he helped Brian Clough's Nottingham Forest win the 1977/78 League Championship. It was a goal fit to win any competition, and it certainly went a long way to cement Villa's control on the destination of the league title. The substitute referee's final whistle was drowned out by the tremendous roar. Surely Villa wouldn't allow their first championship for more than seventy-one years to be thrown away now?

For Albion, Wile, Robertson and Statham had been commanding in defence, while McNaught, along with Allan Evans and Colin Gibson, all had magnificent games. However, the real match glory belonged to Peter Withe, who limped away happily with a dead leg, having set a personal league goal scoring record; he was probably feeling no pain.

Even the most diehard Villa fan must have felt a little pang of sympathy for Albion, who had battled away for almost ninety minutes. Despite this defeat, Albion held onto third place, eight points behind leaders Villa, who were now three points clear of Ipswich.

On the same night, Ipswich beat FC Cologne 1-0 at Portman Road, in the first leg of their UEFA Cup semi-final. In the FA Cup semi-finals, on Saturday 11 April 1981, Manchester City beat Ipswich 1-0 after extra time at Villa Park and Spurs drew 2-2 after extra time with Wolves at Hillsborough. Spurs won the replay 3-0 at Highbury. Ipswich's defeat removed the second part of the domestic treble from their grasp.

Aston Villa: Rimmer, Swain, Gibson, Evans, McNaught, Mortimer, Bremner, Geddis, Withe, Cowans, Morley. Sub: Deacy.

West Bromwich Albion: Godden, Batson, Statham, Moses, Wile, Robertson, Robson B., Brown, Regis, Owen, Barnes. Sub: Mills.

ASTON VILLA v. IPSWICH TOWN

Football League First Division, Villa Park
Referee: Mr B. Hill (Kettering)

Date: Tuesday 14 April 1981
Attendance: 47,495

This game had originally been scheduled to be played two months earlier on 14 February, but had been rearranged twice because of Ipswich's successful cup runs. The Suffolk side returned to Villa Park to play their second game in four days at the old stadium, having lost 1-0 after extra time to Manchester City on Saturday in the semi-final of the FA Cup. Villa had five games left to play, Ipswich six, and three points separated them. Things were looking decidedly bright for the Villans. Saunders recalled Gary Shaw to the starting line-up and, with Gary Williams' hamstring injury clearing up, the defender took over from Allan Evans, who started a two-match suspension. Ipswich welcomed back Frans Thijssen and Paul Mariner, who had both missed the previous league game.

Both sides looked solid and confident at the back but, in the fourth minute, Ken McNaught gifted the lead to Ipswich with a nightmare blunder. Instead of booting clear on the edge of the penalty area, Villa's centre-back unbelievably waited for Jimmy Rimmer to come and collect the ball. Rimmer expected the ball to be pushed back to him. Paul Mariner realised there was a hesitation and sped in to whip the ball away before sliding it to the unmarked Alan Brazil, who stroked it past the helpless Rimmer to put Ipswich one up. It was another moment of madness that had Ron Saunders tearing out what hair he had left. This was just the tonic Ipswich needed after their FA Cup disappointment. Villa were flummoxed as the visitors slipped into the rhythm of safe possession football, stringing together passes back and forth calmly and accurately. Whenever Villa got the ball back, they attacked with power and pace, Morley racing down the left to provide a series of dangerous crosses from which both Peter Withe and Gary Shaw might have scored, but when they broke clear in quick succession, they each shot straight at the advancing 'keeper. Half-time: Villa 0 Ipswich 1.

In the second half, Peter Withe continued his running battle with Terry Butcher and went close with a glancing header that flew narrowly wide. He then repeated the feat a few minutes later, getting ahead of Butcher to power his header just off target. Then Tony Morley went off on a dazzling run down the left before cutting inside to unleash a scorcher that beat Cooper's leap, but flew high over the bar. Villa thought they should have had a penalty midway through the second half when a scything tackle by Russell Osman left Gary Shaw spread-eagled on the ground. Referee Hill shook his head, and waved play on. There was no justice there. Villa were now playing some nice football, and looked dangerous with each attack, but then disaster struck. On seventy-nine minutes, Des Bremner made a complete mess of a pass after winning the ball, kicking it straight to Paul Mariner. The England forward could hardly believe his luck and set off at a pace to the edge of the Villa penalty area, where Gary Williams jockeyed him away from goal. All seemed well

Aston Villa 1	Ipswich Town 2
Shaw (84)	Brazil (4)
	Gates (79)

ASTON VILLA v. IPSWICH TOWN

Tony Morley shoots for goal against Ipswich.

until Mariner fooled everyone with a reverse pass to Eric Gates, who ran forward a few steps to crash an unstoppable shot past Rimmer into the top corner. These stupid mistakes were costing Villa dear. Six minutes from time, Kenny Swain's throw-in was chested to Gary Shaw, who smashed an exceptional volley beyond Cooper to give Villa a small glimmer of hope. The boys in claret and blue threw everything they had left into the attack, but Ipswich's resolute defence, led impressively by Terry Butcher, were determined not to allow Villa a second goal, and the referee's whistle brought this vibrant game to a close. Ipswich had given themselves a chance at the league title in a game that certainly lived up to its billing. There were many moments of sheer magic from both sides, as well as being a marvellous advertisement for hard graft. On another day, Villa might have won comfortably. Certainly Shaw's goal was worthy of being a match-winner. This wasn't Peter Withe's best performance, but remember he and Shaw were playing against two England centre-backs. Withe went close to a couple of goals, but all he got was a booking for trying to kick the ball out of Cooper's hands. John Wark also had his name taken for a foul on Jimmy Rimmer.

ASTON VILLA v. IPSWICH TOWN

Despite this bitter blow, Villa were still one point clear with four matches to play. Ipswich had a game in hand, but they still had to win it.

The First Division table:

	PLD	W	D	L	F	A	PTS
Aston Villa	**38**	**24**	**7**	**7**	**66**	**37**	**55**
Ipswich Town	37	22	10	5	73	35	54
WBA	38	18	11	9	53	37	47
Southampton	38	19	8	11	70	50	46
Liverpool	37	15	15	7	58	39	45
Nottm Forest	38	17	11	10	57	40	45

Gary Shaw celebrated his selection for the England Under-21 squad to play Romania in Swindon on 28 April in bed, after being sent home from training with a cold and high temperature. And Tony Morley was included in the England 'B' squad for the trip to Spain.

Aston Villa: Rimmer, Swain, Gibson, Williams, McNaught, Mortimer, Bremner, Shaw, Withe, Cowans, Morley.
    Sub: Deacy.
Ipswich Town: Cooper, Mills, McCall, Thijssen, Osman, Butcher, Wark, Muhren, Mariner, Brazil, Gates.
    Sub: O'Callaghan.

ASTON VILLA v. NOTTINGHAM FOREST

Football League First Division, Villa Park
Referee: Mr R. Chadwick (Darwen)

Date: Saturday 18 April 1981
Attendance: 34,707

This was a must-win Easter Saturday game for Villa. Forest were without Kenny Burns and Frank Gray, but skipper John McGovern was back after missing ten league games. Gary Shaw had recovered after being sent home on Friday, and was fit to face Forest.

Unchanged Villa raced out of the blocks and, in the first few minutes, created havoc in the Forest defence. First Dave Needham needed to be quick to pip Withe to the ball. Then Einar Aas was forced to head away a dangerous cross from the right. In the third minute, Peter Withe burst into the box between Needham and Aas, but McGovern managed to throw himself in the way of the shot and the ball bounced clear. A minute later, Des Bremner fed Gary Shaw, who was wrestled to the ground by Viv Anderson, who should have been booked, but got away with a lecture. Then Shaw was given offside twice in succession as he raced onto long balls from midfield. Trevor Francis gave the ball away to Tony Morley in the ninth minute. The winger swerved round Anderson and Mills before swinging in a corker of a cross that set off a frenetic goalmouth melée, with boots flying in every direction until the ball was finally hacked away.

Forest ended twelve minutes of Villa domination when Peter Ward hit the byline to whip in a low cross that was met perfectly by Trevor Francis. But the first million-pound player ballooned his first-time shot over the bar. Colin Gibson took a knock which needed the trainer's attention. Villa could consider themselves robbed in the nineteenth minute. At the end of a great run, Tony Morley crossed from the left and everybody in Villa Park, except the referee and his linesman, saw Viv Anderson handle the ball. Just after this incident Trevor Francis looked puzzled by the huge cheers from the Villa fans when he missed Peter Ward's cross. The cheers were for the news, flashed on the electric scoreboard, that Arsenal had gone a goal up at Ipswich.

A twenty-third-minute midfield collision left Gary Mills with blood pouring from a nasty gash to his right eyebrow. He was forced to leave the field with a sponge clamped to the wound. Ten-man Forest drew everyone back behind the ball. But in the twenty-ninth minute it all came right for the league leaders. Morley sped off on another brilliant run down the left. His perfect pass into the box found Des Bremner, who was blatantly pushed in the back by Bryn Gunn. Referee Chadwick had no hesitation and pointed to the spot. As Gordon Cowans spotted the ball, the tension in the crowd grew appreciably. After all, he had missed the last penalty he had taken. There were no problems this time, however, as the midfielder coolly slid the ball past Peter Shilton. The crowd went crackers, and rightly so. Mills returned to the fray a couple of minutes later, to discover his side were 1-0 down, and almost immediately it might have been 2-0. Withe played a one-two with Mortimer, to tee-up a clear thirty-third-minute chance that the Villa skipper scooped over the top. Four minutes later, Forest might have equalised. Francis' left-wing cross was sliced to Peter Ward by Colin Gibson, but the

---

Aston Villa 2
  Cowans (penalty, 29)
  Withe (45)

Nottingham Forest 0

Gordon Cowans beats Trevor Francis to the ball.

former Burton Albion striker's shot hit Gibson's outstretched boot and spun over Rimmer's crossbar. Then, with half-time approaching, Francis sprinted down the left to deliver an in-swinging cross that forced Rimmer to palm the ball over the bar. John Robertson's flag-kick was met by Needham, but he didn't connect properly and Rimmer gathered comfortably. In the forty-fifth minute, Villa scored a second. Tony Morley swept down the left wing and crossed to the far post, where the unmarked Peter Withe powered a firm header past Shilton. Half-time: Villa 2 Forest 0.

The speed of Villa's attacking didn't let up one bit in the second half. They began with a tremendous three-man move involving Morley and Shaw, who set up Mortimer for a first-time crackerjack that again flew over the bar. In the fifty-first minute, another incisive thrust almost brought a goal. Shilton pushed a Tony Morley in-swinger straight to Shaw, but Aas was able to whip the ball away as Shaw shaped to shoot. Forest hit back in the fifty-fourth minute. Viv Anderson galloped into the area to unleash a shot that had Rimmer scrambling across his goal to parry the ball back to the England full-back, who smashed the rebound into the side-netting.

On the hour mark, news came through that Arsenal had scored a second goal at Ipswich and Villa Park erupted with pleasure. Buoyed by this fabulous news, Villa went for the jugular. Tony Morley was unlucky not to score a third Villa goal after a trademark dash down the left. The winger cut inside to crash in what looked like an unstoppable shot, until Shilton launched his body into the air to make a fantastic leaping save. Next, Shilton bravely threw himself at the ball as Cowans and Swain swung their boots at Withe's flicked pass. Then, in the sixty-ninth minute, Shaw met Cowans' corner to force an incredible instinctive save from Peter Shilton. In the seventy-third minute, Tony

Aston Villa v. Nottingham Forest

Morley wasted one of the best chances of the game when, with only Shilton to beat he hesitated instead of shooting first-time, allowing Forest to get the ball away. In the final minutes Peter Shilton left no one in doubt that he was the best goalkeeper in England by once again denying Villa a certain goal with a tremendous reflex save. Peter Withe headed on Morley's corner to Ken McNaught, who sent a close-range bullet header towards the corner of the net. Amazingly, the Forest 'keeper threw up his hands to knock the ball down, before grabbing it at the second attempt.

This was a fantastic performance by Villa and, with Ipswich losing 2-0 at home to Arsenal, things were looking mighty good. Three more wins and the title was Villa's.

The First Division table:

	PLD	W	D	L	F	A	PTS
Aston Villa	**39**	**25**	**7**	**7**	**68**	**37**	**57**
Ipswich Town	38	22	10	6	73	37	54
Southampton	39	19	9	11	72	52	47
WBA	39	18	11	10	54	39	47
Arsenal	39	16	15	8	54	42	47
Liverpool	38	15	16	7	58	39	46

Aston Villa: Rimmer, Swain, Gibson, Williams, McNaught, Mortimer, Bremner, Shaw, Withe, Cowans, Morley. Sub: Deacy.

Nottingham Forest: Shilton, Anderson, Gray F., McGovern, Aas, Needham, Mills, Ward, Francis, Gray S., Robertson. Sub: Walsh.

STOKE CITY v. ASTON VILLA

Football League First Division, The Victoria Ground
Referee: Mr P.N. Willis (Macclesfield)

Date: Monday 20 April 1981
Attendance: 23,511

Allan Evans returned after his two-match suspension to an otherwise unchanged Villa side for their third game in seven days. Mid-table Stoke had Dutch winger Loek Ursem back at number seven, to provide the ammunition for England Under-21 international Adrian Heath and 15-goal frontman Lee Chapman. The bone-hard Victoria Ground pitch promised some rare thrills with an unpredictable bounce of the ball.

Both teams began lethargically in a dour affair that only occasionally sparked into enough life to lift the modest-sized crowd. Maybe too many Easter eggs had been consumed? This was hard work indeed; functional rather than fancy football. Youngster Adrian Heath tested Jimmy Rimmer, who rose to the occasion marvellously, with an instinctive save. Then when Stoke won a corner, the Villa goalkeeper pulled off a great reflex save to keep out a powerful header from free-scoring striker-turned-defender Brendan O'Callaghan. In the early stages O'Callaghan certainly kept Peter Withe quiet but, in the end, couldn't stop him from grabbing a goal. Villa took the lead in the twenty-second minute with a nicely worked goal from Withe; his nineteenth league goal of the season. The big striker had certainly made a huge difference since his summer transfer from Newcastle. His battling displays earned him almost folklore status with the Villa fans, who appreciated his tremendous contribution to the side. His goals and his brave competitive instinct had inspired the rest of the team, particularly Gary Shaw, whose talent had blossomed alongside Withe. The goal was the result of a lot of hard graft, and the pity was that Villa failed to hang onto it for longer than three minutes.

In the twenty-fifth minute, Stoke won a left-wing corner, which Paul Maguire swung into the near post, where Brendan O'Callaghan glanced a header past Rimmer. Although the ball appeared to have taken a touch off a defender's head on its way into the net, the goal was awarded to O'Callaghan; his seventh of the season. The midfield battle intensified with the ball bouncing all over the place on the rock-hard surface, often making ball control nigh-on impossible. Ursem tried a few dangerous runs, but Colin Gibson kept a tight reign on the Dutchman to nullify his threat. Mortimer worked tirelessly alongside his two cohorts Bremner and Cowans, who tried constantly to get Morley away on the left. However, this was proving to be one of the least effective displays of wing-play from Villa's number eleven. So far, Ken McNaught had been able to keep twenty-one-year-old Lee Chapman fairly quiet, and Allan Evans worked tirelessly in his comeback to cope with the impressive free-running of twenty-year-old Adrian Heath. Half-time: 1-1.

At the start of the second half, Gary Shaw was gifted a great opportunity, but the out-of-sorts youngster contrived to miss the chance to regain the lead for Villa. Eventually, Saunders replaced the twenty-year-old striker with substitute Eamonn Deacy. Mike Doyle turned in agony when his

Stoke City 1	Aston Villa 1
O'Callaghan (25)	Withe (22)

STOKE CITY v. ASTON VILLA

Ken McNaught in action.

powerful downward header was cleared off the goal line. However, Villa's defence managed to hold out against a late Stoke surge, to take one point from the game. They certainly didn't deserve anything less. Stoke had a few chances but, fortunately for the league leaders, both Heath and Bracewell were guilty of dragging shots the wrong side of Rimmer's post when they might have done better. Referee Willis and his linesmen had a controversy-free afternoon, with both sides showing good sportsmanship without compromising the firmness of their tackling. Villa's boss, delighted with the point, reminded reporters that the game of football is also about fighting and battling, outstanding attributes that some people knock. Villa had these qualities in abundance, as well as the skill to capitalise on those priceless assets.

Easter 1981 had proved to be great for Villa. Two points against Nottingham Forest and one against Stoke went a long way to wiping out the memory of gifting Ipswich two goals and with them both points. This compared well with the fortunes of their main rival for the title, who lost both their Easter games and with that surely a realistic chance of winning the championship. The taste in Villa mouths was sweet, in contrast to the bitterness of Bobby Robson and his side. Ipswich had thrown away a possible once-in-a-lifetime opportunity by losing 2-0 to Arsenal and 1-0 to Norwich after beating Villa a mere seven days before. The feeling must have been awful. The pressure had finally told on one of the title contenders. Of the other leading clubs, West Bromwich Albion, Arsenal and Forest all won, Southampton drew, and reigning champions Liverpool didn't play.

The First Division table:

	PLD	W	D	L	F	A	PTS
Aston Villa	**40**	**25**	**8**	**7**	**69**	**38**	**58**
Ipswich Town	39	22	10	7	73	38	54
WBA	40	19	11	10	56	40	49
Arsenal	40	17	15	8	57	44	49
Southampton	40	19	10	11	73	53	48
Nottm Forest	40	18	11	11	58	42	47

On Wednesday 22 April, Ipswich wiped away some of their sadness by beating FC Cologne 1-0 in the second leg of their UEFA Cup semi-final in Germany to reach the final 2-0 on aggregate.

Stoke City: Fox, Evans, Munro, Dodd, O'Callaghan, Doyle, Ursem, Bracewell, Chapman, Heath, Maguire.
  Sub: Hampton.
Aston Villa: Rimmer, Swain, Gibson, Evans, McNaught, Mortimer, Bremner, Shaw (Deacy), Withe, Cowans, Morley.

ASTON VILLA v. MIDDLESBROUGH

Football League First Division, Villa Park   **Date:** Saturday 25 April 1981
Referee: Mr M. Dimblebee (Stevenage)   **Attendance:** 38,018

Gary Shaw returned to the unchanged Villa line-up for this crucial final home game of the season. In the last three seasons, the Teessiders had proved to be a bit of a bogey team on their visits to Villa Park. Beleaguered Middlesbrough boss John Neal brought in uncompromising full-back John Craggs, teenage midfielder Colin Ross and Yugoslavian striker Bozo Jankovic after injury. Billy Ashcroft was selected at centre half in place of Mike Angus, who was dropped after Boro had been beaten 1-0 at home by Coventry on Tuesday.

On the bitterly cold afternoon, determined Villa set out to dominate Boro and created havoc in the visitors' defence. Villa won a free-kick that Ken McNaught floated into the box, where Allan Evans forced a marvellous reflex save from Jim Platt with a powerful downward header, the Boro 'keeper diving low to his right to palm the ball away. Villa were fabulous, seemingly unperturbed by the swirling wind and freezing rain. Morley left Craggs for dead to find Shaw with a neat cross. However, the youngster's tame header dropped to Ian Bailey, who hacked the ball upfield. In the ninth minute Peter Withe sent Morley away again and this time Gary Shaw met his cross perfectly to send in a powerful downward header that bounced straight into Platt's arms. A few minutes later Platt produced another top-drawer diving save to deny Colin Gibson. The full-back controlled Withe's return pass in the area to drill in a crackerjack that the Middlesbrough 'keeper saved low at the foot of his right-hand post. Platt followed up his fifteen-minute one-man show with another brilliant save to keep out a stunning Peter Withe effort. At the other end, all Jimmy Rimmer had to do was take one or two goal-kicks, and field the occasional back-pass.

When Billy Ashcroft floored Withe with a crude tackle in the penalty area, referee Dimblebee unbelievably shook his head to deny Villa a penalty. Boro's sole effort came on twenty minutes, when Mark Proctor surged to the edge of the area only to thump his shot well wide. Three minutes later Villa went one up. Craggs found a way to stop Morley, flooring the winger on the left touchline. The resultant free-kick was swung deep to Evans, who headed the ball into the danger zone. Withe touched it to Gary Shaw, who bent the ball around Platt into the top corner. A fabulous goal that announced that Shaw was back in business. John Craggs must have been heartily fed up with the sight of Tony Morley. On the winger's next thrilling run, Craggs' flying boot missed, and Morley was away again, swerving inside before slipping the ball to Shaw, who flicked the ball across to Peter Withe. This time, the striker's curler flew narrowly wide. In the thirty-third minute Shaw sent Gibson on an overlapping run before whipping over a perfect cross that Withe crashed against the post with a great header. Then Withe chipped the ball left towards Morley, where Craggs' latest strategy was to pull the ball down with his hand, and a booking followed. The free-kick fell to the edge of the box, where Gary Shaw turned and shot in one movement but unfortunately Platt caught the ball with a

Aston Villa 3   **Middlesbrough 0**
Shaw (23)
Withe (51)
Evans (80)

ASTON VILLA v. MIDDLESBROUGH

Ron Saunders watches from the dugout.

tremendous leap. Just after, Des Bremner's centre reached the unmarked Morley via neat touches by Withe and Shaw, but the winger opted for power over accuracy, and smashed his shot high into the crowd. Three minutes before the break, Swain surged into the right of the area to crash in a blistering shot that Platt could only push into Morley's path. Sadly the winger hadn't learned anything from his last effort and, with an open goal facing him, blasted the ball high and wide. On forty-five minutes Morley tried to make amends during a frantic melée inside Boro's goalmouth. But again, his full-bloodied exocet failed to find its intended target, after Withe's piledriver had been blocked. Half-time: Villa 1 Boro 0.

Villa began the second half with a couple of incisive attacks that brought Platt into action again. The Ulster-born 'keeper gratefully grabbed Cowans' through ball from Withe. Then Shaw lobbed the ball into his arms instead of over the 'keeper's head. Seconds later, Platt was pleased to watch Withe's left-foot curler skim the bar. Another goal just had to come, and it did six minutes after the restart. Cowans and Morley tricked Craggs and Ross near the left-hand corner. Morley lifted the ball into the middle, where Peter Withe out-jumped the defenders to power a firm header past Platt. The noise coming from Villa Park was enough to stop the traffic in New Street; however, the news that Ipswich were one up against Manchester City dampened some of the cheers.

Only the brilliance of Jim Platt had prevented Villa from being at least five ahead, and he did it again in the next three attacks. The big 'keeper put Gordon Cowans off, and the midfielder headed over. Then Morley had a shot blocked and, when Mortimer cracked in a beauty, Platt was on hand

ASTON VILLA v. MIDDLESBROUGH

again with yet another diving save. Middlesbrough finally managed a shot in the sixty-fifth minute, but Ross' strike from the edge of the area ricocheted behind for a corner and, although that came to nothing, eight minutes later Boro tried again through McAndrew, who hit his shot straight at Jimmy Rimmer.

In the eightieth minute, Villa scored a cracker of a third goal. Mortimer swung over a corner that Ashcroft failed to clear. The ball dropped to Allan Evans, who smashed a scorcher past Platt. In the dying minutes, Tony Morley went close, with a delightful thirty-yard chip-shot that beat Platt's athletic leap, only to scrape the top of the bar.

Ipswich kept their title hopes alive with a 1-0 victory at home to Manchester City. They had two games left to play, were four points behind, and had one game in hand on Villa, plus a slightly better goal difference. They still had an outside chance of winning the title. The fight for the following season's UEFA Cup places had hotted-up to melting point. Arsenal jumped to third with a 3-1 victory at Wolves, Forest won, Liverpool drew and dropped to eighth, Southampton lost and West Bromwich Albion didn't play.

The First Division table:

	PLD	W	D	L	F	A	PTS
Aston Villa	**41**	**26**	**8**	**7**	**72**	**38**	**60**
Ipswich Town	40	23	10	7	74	38	56
Arsenal	41	18	15	8	59	45	51
Nottm Forest	41	19	11	11	61	43	49
WBA	40	19	11	10	56	40	49
Southampton	41	19	10	12	73	54	48

Aston Villa: Rimmer, Swain, Gibson, Evans, McNaught, Mortimer, Bremner, Shaw, Withe, Cowans, Morley. Sub: Deacy.

Middlesbrough: Platt, Craggs, Bailey, Ross, Ashcroft, McAndrew, Cochrane, Proctor, Shearer, Jankovic, Armstrong. Sub: Askew.

ARSENAL v. ASTON VILLA

Football League First Division, Highbury
Referee: Mr D. Hutchinson (Bourn, Cambs)

Date: Saturday 2 May 1981
Attendance: 57,472

A draw was all Villa needed to take the title. However, standing in their way was a Gunners side on a roll, unbeaten in their last eight games, and always eager to shoot down any complacent visitors to Highbury. Arsenal had former Wolves wonder-kid Alan Sunderland back in the side, with John Hollins moving to number two in place of John Devine. Villa were unchanged for the third game in a row. A mass exodus from Birmingham resulted in gridlock all around Highbury as a record convoy of seventy-one coaches, organised by the Villa travel club, was escorted to the stadium at snail's pace by a large number of police. Many fans without tickets queued for hours to support their heroes in this championship decider. The entire Clock End of the ground was taken over by Villa fans but, sad to say, five minutes before kick-off, this wonderful occasion was marred by a pitched battle. A horde of Villa fans raced from the Clock End to challenge Arsenal fans storming from the West Stand. Thankfully the police soon gained control and a number of fans were arrested. Hopefully Highbury's extra-special visitor, legendary Brazilian striker Pelé, who was at the ground on a promotional tour, had not witnessed the disgraceful scenes. Just before kick-off, the world's greatest-ever footballer was presented to the crowd, who responded with an enormous reception for the great man. Then hundreds of multi-coloured balloons were released from the centre circle, to welcome the teams onto the pitch, flanked by scores of police, who were now also stationed all around the perimeter of the pitch.

Arsenal kicked-off a couple of minutes later and immediately lost the ball. Villa swept into the Gunners' half and won a corner on the right. Dennis Mortimer swung the ball in and Pat Jennings leaped high to fist the ball away. On three minutes, Ken McNaught thumped a long free-kick upfield to Peter Withe but, with Jennings sprinting from his line, the striker spooned his shot over the crossbar. Then Des Bremner fired in a twenty-yard left-foot curler that spun behind off a defender for a corner. The flag-kick ran loose to Mortimer, who completely missed his kick and Tony Morley, following up, blasted the ball way over the top. In the eleventh minute, Villa went a goal down. Arsenal were awarded a free-kick on the left when Bremner impeded Davis. Davis swung over a near-post free-kick that Sunderland headed on to Willie Young, who drove a vicious left-foot shot into the bottom left-hand corner of Rimmer's net. The goal signalled more trouble in the crowd at the Clock End, but police rushed into the multitude to make a number of arrests.

For the next ten minutes, Arsenal were in total control. Then, on twenty-one minutes, Villa broke forward. Evans headed down McNaught's long free-kick to Withe, but the striker's first-timer flew over the crossbar. In the twenty-fourth minute, from another McNaught free-kick, Evans nodded tamely into Jennings' arms. The trouble at the Clock End flared up again, and extra police were called in to calm the situation. On thirty-three minutes, after Cowans had fired a speculative twenty-five-

Arsenal 2
Young (11)
McDermott (44)

Aston Villa 0

ARSENAL v. ASTON VILLA

Pat Jennings punches clear from Withe and Shaw.

yarder well wide, the Gunners swept upfield again, and had the Villa defence at sixes and sevens. Brian McDermott wasted a great opportunity to extend Arsenal's slender lead after Stapleton had put him clear with a neat back-header. With only Rimmer to beat, the twenty-year-old completely miskicked. The news that Ipswich were leading Middlesbrough 1-0 at Ayresome Park added to Villa's woeful afternoon. Then, a minute before the interval, things went from bad to worse when Villa won a rare corner. Pat Jennings fisted Mortimer's flag-kick clear, and Nicholas booted the ball upfield to Brian McDermott, who shrugged off Swain and Gibson, before shooting low past Rimmer into the right-hand corner of the net. Villa were dead and buried, needing a miracle of Lazarus-like proportions if they were going to take anything from this game. Half-time: Arsenal 2 Villa 0.

Ron Saunders' half-time words of wisdom obviously had a positive effect and Villa had a go at Arsenal for a few short minutes. Morley looked refreshed, and broke down the left only to be halted by an excellent tackle by John Hollins. Then Peter Withe tried to lob the ball over Jennings, but was hopelessly off target. Five minutes after the interval, there was a bizarre incident to say the least. Referee Hutchinson awarded a free-kick to Villa. Naturally all Villa's players moved to an attacking formation but, before they could take the kick, the referee changed his mind and gave the kick to Arsenal, who took it quickly, and only the linesman's offside flag saved Villa.

As the clock moved inexorably towards the hour mark, Withe set up a chance for Shaw, but the youngster's volley spun well wide. Then the news that Middlesbrough had equalised against Ipswich drew a huge chorus of cheers from the Villa faithful. A Villa defeat and an Ipswich draw would still see Villa take the title. Alan Sunderland was booked for stupidly kicking the ball away and, suddenly, there were small signs that Arsenal might be easing up a little. Before Villa could stage a comeback, Arsenal went close again. Brian Talbot headed narrowly over the bar, crashing heads with Bremner in the process. Talbot got to his feet rubbing his shoulder but, with blood pouring from his head, Bremner rushed off the pitch to have the wound treated. In the seventieth minute, Pat Jennings tipped Cowans' twenty-five-yarder over the bar for safety. Patched up Des Bremner returned to the fray before the corner could be taken and, shortly after, Talbot had to leave the field with a shoulder injury; Sammy Nelson substituting. Then, in the seventy-fifth minute, Peter Withe produced Villa's best effort with a great turn and swerving shot from just inside the area that Jennings caught with a great leap. Arsenal seemed content to absorb everything Villa could throw at them in the final minutes, without allowing the visitors the space to create any real chances. The referee blew his whistle to bring to an end a fabulous season for Aston Villa. A pity Villa couldn't have at least got a draw, but in the end it all proved to be academic with the news that Middlesbrough had beaten Ipswich 2-1. The fingernails of the Villa fans had most probably been bitten down to the quick while they waited for the Ipswich result to filter through, but when it did they literally went wild. Their team had won the First Division championship for the first time in seventy-one years. The claret-and-blue half of Birmingham could now celebrate officially. Villa had won the league title for the first time since 1909/10. **Aston Villa – League Champions 1980/81.**

Ipswich had lost seven of their final ten league games, picking up only six points out of a possible twenty. Obviously fighting for glory in both the league and the UEFA Cup had taken its toll.

The First Division table:

	PLD	W	D	L	F	A	PTS
Aston Villa	**42**	**26**	**8**	**8**	**72**	**40**	**60**
Ipswich Town	41	23	10	8	75	40	56
Arsenal	42	19	15	8	61	45	53
WBA	41	20	11	10	60	42	51
Nottm Forest	42	19	12	11	62	44	50
Southampton	41	19	10	12	73	54	48

Villa's triumphant season sparked a number of awards: Brian Little received the Midlands Soccer Writers' Merit award, ATV's Billy Wright presented Gary Shaw with the Midlands Young Player of the Year award, Peter Withe was named New Midlands Player of the year and Ron Saunders received the *Evening Mail* Sports Personality of the Month award for April with a smile. Other accolades for Villa personnel were as follows: Gary Shaw was named Young Player of the Year, Ron Saunders was Bell's Football Manager of the Year, having won the Manager of the Month in October 1980 and Kenny Swain, Allan Evans and Gary Shaw were selected by the PFA in the First Division XI.

Arsenal: Jennings, Hollins, Sansom, Talbot (Nelson), O'Leary, Young, McDermott, Sunderland, Stapleton, Nicholas, Davis.
Aston Villa: Rimmer; Swain, Gibson; Evans, McNaught, Mortimer; Bremner, Shaw, Withe, Cowans, Morley. Sub: Deacy.

Postscript

On Wednesday 6 May Ipswich won the first leg of their UEFA Cup final against Dutch Champions AZ67 Alkmaar of Amsterdam, by three goals to nil.

On 12 May Peter Withe played for the full England side at Wembley, in the 1-0 defeat at the hands of Brazil. Zico scored the winner in this friendly international. The teams were: England: Clemence, Neal, Sansom, Robson, Martin, Wilkins, Coppell, McDermott, Withe, Rix, Barnes. Brazil: Valdir, Edevaldo, Isidoro, Luisinho, Cerezo, Junior, Oscar, Socrates, Reinaldo, Zico, Eder.

On Wednesday 13 May, Ipswich's already ended dream of championship glory was dealt a final blow with a 3-2 home defeat at the hands of Southampton. Seven days later they gained some consolation when they won the UEFA Cup by beating AZ67 Alkmaar 5-4 on aggregate, despite losing the away leg in Holland 4-2. Also on 13 May Dynamo Tbilisi beat Carl Zeiss Jena 2-1 in Düsseldorf to win the European Cup Winners' Cup.

In the FA Cup final replay at Wembley on 14 May Tottenham beat Manchester City 3-2 after the first game, on 9 May, had been drawn 1-1. Liverpool wrapped up the final league game of the season with a 1-0 win over Manchester City on 19 May.

On 20 May, Peter Withe played for England at Wembley, in the goal-less draw with Wales in the British International Championship game. The teams: England: Corrigan, Anderson, Sansom, Robson, Watson, Wilkins, Coppell, Hoddle, Withe (Woodcock), Rix, Barnes. Wales: Davies, Jones, Ratcliffe, Nicholas, Phillips, Price, Harris (Giles), Flynn, Walsh, Thomas, James L. (Rush).

Three days later, on 23 May, Withe played again for England in the British International Championship at Wembley. This time, England lost 1-0 to Scotland, courtesy of a John Robertson penalty. England: Corrigan, Anderson, Sansom, Wilkins, Watson (Martin), Robson, Coppell, Hoddle, Withe, Rix, Woodcock (Francis). Scotland: Rough, Stewart, Gray F., McGrain, McLeish, Miller, Provan (Sturrock), Archibald, Jordan, Hartford (Narey), Robertson.

The final European competition was wrapped up on 27 May, when Liverpool beat Real Madrid 1-0 in Paris to win the European Cup. The Reds had faded towards the end of the season to finish in fifth position, and had to make do with two trophies, the League Cup and the European Cup.

Gary Shaw played for England in the UEFA Under-21 Championship 0-0 draw against Switzerland in Neufchatel on 31 May. Then, on 5 June, in Keszthely versus Hungary, England won 2-1 with goals from Shaw and Fashanu.

So that was it, Aston Villa were officially crowned champions of England. They had played the best and had beaten the best. In 42 League games, they had won 26, drawn 8, and had only been beaten on 8 occasions, winning the championship four points ahead of runners-up Ipswich. Peter Withe finished as the First Division's joint-top goalscorer with Spurs' Steve Archibald, with 20 league goals apiece. Gary Shaw was joint-third with 18 league goals. And Villa's average league attendance was 33,641. The next season would see Aston Villa play in the European Cup for the first time ever. A season to remember indeed. **Aston Villa – First Division Champions 1980/81.**

1980/81 Statistics

1980/81 final top three league placings:

	PLD	W	D	L	F	A	W	D	L	F	A	PTS
Aston Villa	**42**	**16**	**3**	**2**	**40**	**13**	**10**	**5**	**6**	**32**	**27**	**60**
Ipswich	42	15	4	2	45	14	8	6	7	32	29	56
Arsenal	42	13	8	0	36	17	6	7	8	25	28	53

West Bromwich Albion finished fourth and Liverpool fifth, with 52 and 51 points respectively. Sixth were Southampton, with Nottingham Forest seventh. Crystal Palace finished bottom of the league and were relegated to the Second Division, along with Leicester and Norwich.

Seven Villa players played in every game in the league, League Cup and FA Cup that season: Jimmy Rimmer; Kenny Swain; Ken McNaught; Dennis Mortimer; Des Bremner; Gordon Cowans and Tony Morley. This was a fantastic tribute to the fitness levels that Ron Saunders and his team had maintained throughout the season.

Villa celebrate the championship in the Highbury dressing room.

1980/81 STATISTICS

The Players:

Jimmy Rimmer, *goalkeeper (42 League appearances; 1 appearance in the FA Cup; 3 in the League Cup).*

Jimmy was an outstanding goalkeeper, joining Aston Villa from Arsenal for a bargain fee of £65,000 in August 1977. Following his league debut on 20 August 1977 in the 2-1 away victory at QPR, he went on to make 287 appearances for the Villans between 1977 and 1983. Jimmy was born in Southport on 10 February 1948, starting his career at Manchester United as an amateur and apprentice, making his league debut in 1968. Thirty-four first-team league appearances followed, before he moved to Swansea on loan, where he made 17 appearances. In February 1974 Arsenal paid £40,000 for him. Jimmy played 124 league games for the Gunners. He won a single full England cap in May 1976, in the 3-2 victory over Italy in New York, plus two Under-23 caps.

Aside from playing all 42 league matches in Villa's championship-winning season, Jimmy is also famously (or is it infamously?) remembered for his brief appearance in the final of the European Cup the following season, having to leave the field with a back injury, his place being taken by Nigel Spink. From Villa, he joined Swansea City in August 1983. Then for a time he played in Malta, before finally hanging up his gloves after making well in excess of 500 appearances in his career. He was coach at Swansea in season 1987/88.

Kenny Swain, *right-back (42 League appearances; 1 appearance in the FA Cup; 3 in the League Cup).*

Born in Birkenhead on 28 January 1952, Kenny signed schoolboy forms for Bolton Wanderers, before joining Wycombe Wanderers as an amateur. In 1973 he joined Chelsea on professional forms, where he played in 114 league games, plus five as substitute, scoring 26 goals. From Stamford Bridge, he transferred to Villa for a fee of around £100,000 in December 1978, making his league debut on 16 December 1978 in a 1-1 draw with Norwich City at Villa Park. After a short loan period with the Baggies he went on to make 179 appearances for the Villans, scoring five goals. He subsequently moved to Nottingham Forest in 1982, then to Portsmouth in July 1985.

A member of Villa's 1982 European Cup-winning side, Kenny Swain was a highly rated full-back, and had the distinction of playing in two promotion-winning sides: Portsmouth in 1986/87 from the Second Division, and Crewe Alexandra from the Fourth Division in 1988/89, where he subsequently became player/coach and then assistant manager. He was appointed manager of Wigan Athletic for 1993/94 before moving to Grimsby Town as reserve team coach and assistant manager in 1995, and caretaker manager in October 1996 until May 1997. Kenny was another who made well in excess of 500 appearances in his career.

Colin Gibson, *left-back (19 League appearances, plus 2 as substitute; 3 appearances in the League Cup)*.

Born in Bridport on 6 April 1960, Colin signed amateur forms for Portsmouth before moving to Aston Villa as a trainee in July 1976. He signed professional forms in April 1978, making his league debut on 18 November 1978 in a 2-0 victory over Bristol City at Villa Park. Colin went on to make 238 appearances for Villa, scoring 17 goals. In November 1985, he transferred to Manchester United where he made 95 appearances. Towards the end of his time at Old Trafford, Colin was loaned out for a couple of months to Port Vale, before being transferred to Leicester City in December 1990. The Foxes granted him a free transfer to Blackpool in September 1994, and he ended his career as a one-season, non-contract player at Walsall in 1996. On the international stage he won caps for England at Youth, Under-21 and 'B' level.

Gary Williams, *left-back (21 League appearances, plus 1 as substitute; 1 appearance in the FA Cup)*.

Gary was born in Wolverhampton on 17 June 1960, and joined Villa as an apprentice in July 1976, turning professional in June 1978, making his league debut against Everton at Villa Park in a 1-1 draw. Mainly known as a left-back, Gary was comfortable in a wide variety of positions. In a professional career spanning sixteen years, he made more than 500 appearances, including 303 for Villa, scoring two goals. In a short loan spell at Walsall in 1980 he helped the Saddlers gain promotion from the Fourth Division.

After winning the League Championship, European Cup and Super Cup with Villa, he joined Leeds United in July 1987, staying with the Yorkshire club until moving to Watford in January 1990. Gary ended his playing career at Bradford City in 1994, having joined them in December 1991.

Eamonn Deacy, *left-back (5 League appearances, plus 4 as substitute)*.

Eamonn Deacy was born in the Irish city of Galway on 1 October 1958, signing for Aston Villa from Galway Rovers in March 1979. Unfortunately for Eamonn, he joined Villa at a time when they had an abundance of riches at left-back, forcing the Irishman to have to be content with an understudy role whenever Colin Gibson or Gary Williams were unfit. He made 40 senior appearances, including 10 as substitute, in which time he scored one goal. In October 1983 he went on loan to Derby County, where he made five appearances, returning to his home city in July 1984, to play for Galway United. He won four international caps for the Republic of Ireland.

1980/81 STATISTICS

Allan Evans, *centre-back (39 League appearances, 7 League goals; 1 appearance in the FA Cup; 3 appearances in the League Cup)*.

Allan Evans was born in Polbeath, near Edinburgh on 12 October 1956. A stalwart of Villa's defence, he began his career as a striker, before being successfully converted into a solid and reliable centre-back. His football journey started at Dunfermline Athletic in 1972 as an apprentice, turning professional in October 1973. He was transferred to Aston Villa in June 1977, making his league debut in the 0-0 draw at Villa Park with Leicester City on 4 March 1978. He went on to make 469 senior appearances, scoring 60 goals in a thirteen-year Villa Park career. In August 1989, he moved to Leicester on a free transfer, before making a trip down under to play for Brisbane United in 1990. On his return to England, he signed for Darlington in March 1991, ending his playing career in May of the same year. A month later, he accepted the post of assistant manager to Brian Little at Leicester and then, of course, followed his former colleague to Aston Villa in 1994, then to Stoke City in 1998 and West Bromwich Albion in 1999. In 2000 Allan didn't follow Little to Hull City, but branched out into management with Greenock Morton, until getting the axe in January 2001.

Strangely Allan Evans was only selected by Scotland on four occasions.

Ken McNaught, *centre-back (42 League appearances; 1 appearance in the FA Cup; 3 appearances in the League Cup)*.

Born in Kirkcaldy on 11 January 1955, Ken McNaught was a solid defender, hard, but skilful. His reputation of being short on discipline long gone, he played in every one of Villa's 46 competitive games in 1980/81. Joining Everton as a junior in July 1970, Ken turned professional in May 1972, making 64 league appearances for the Toffees, plus two as substitute, scoring three goals. He was transferred to Aston Villa for a reported fee of £200,000 in July 1977 and made his debut on the same day as Jimmy Rimmer, 20 August 1977, at QPR in a 1-1 draw. He went on to appear 260 times for the Villa first team, weighing in with 13 goals. In August 1983, Ken was transferred to West Bromwich Albion for £125,000, where he notched up more than 100 senior games. After a brief loan spell with Manchester City, he moved to Sheffield United in July 1985, retiring from the playing side of the game in May 1986.

He accepted a coaching position with Dunfermline Athletic in 1986, subsequently moving to Swansea City as assistant manager.

Des Bremner, *midfield (42 League appearances, 2 goals; 1 appearance in the FA Cup; 3 appearances in the League Cup)*.

Born in Aberchirder, Scotland, on 7 September 1952, Des Bremner signed for Hibernian in 1971, turning professional in November 1972, before transferring to Aston Villa in September 1979. After making his league debut on 2 September 1979 in the 0-0 draw with Arsenal at Villa Park, he went on to make 277 senior appearances for Villa, scoring 10 goals. In October 1984, he moved across the city to Birmingham, where he once again became a stalwart of the first team, signing for Fulham in August 1989 before moving back to the Midlands, first with Walsall for a few months between March and May 1990, then to Stafford Rangers until 1992, returning to Villa Park in 1999 to work as a coach.

For Scotland, Des won 1 full cap, to add to the 9 he won with the Scottish Under-23 side.

Dennis Mortimer, *midfield (42 League appearances, 4 goals; 1 appearance in the FA Cup; 3 appearances in the League Cup).*

Dennis Mortimer was born in Liverpool on 5 April 1952, signing apprentice forms for Coventry City in June 1967, where he made 192 League appearances, scoring 10 goals. He was transferred to Aston Villa in December 1975 for a fee in the region of £175,000. Dennis made his debut in the 4-1 destruction of West Ham United at Villa Park on 26 December 1975 and became one of Ron Saunders' key players at Villa. As captain, he drove the team forward to League Cup success in 1976/77, the title of 1980/81 and the European and Super Cups in the following seasons. He went on to make 406 appearances for Villa, scoring 36 goals.

A dynamic and powerful midfielder, Dennis Mortimer graced many stadia all over the world, but surprisingly was never capped by England at full level. He had to content himself with three England 'B' caps, plus six appearances for England Under-23s, and six outings at Youth level.

Dennis Mortimer shows the trophy to the Villa fans.

1980/81 Statistics

After a spell on loan at Sheffield United in 1984, Dennis joined Brighton, and then Birmingham City, before moving to non-league Kettering Town, and then Redditch as player-manager.

Gordon Cowans, *midfield (42 League appearances, 5 goals (4 penalties); 1 appearance in the FA Cup; 3 appearances in the League Cup).*

One of Aston Villa's greats, 'Sid' Cowans was born in Cornforth, County Durham, on 27 October 1958. He signed apprentice forms for Villa in July 1974, and made his debut when he came on as substitute in the 2-1 victory over Manchester City at Maine Road on 7 February 1976. A wonderfully talented footballer, he made 528 first-team appearances, scoring 59 goals for Aston Villa in three separate spells with the club, in which time he won the League Cup, the European Cup and European Super Cup, plus of course, the league championship.

In June 1985 he was transferred to the Italian club Bari along with Paul Rideout for a combined fee approaching £1 million. He rejoined Villa in July 1988, reputedly for around £250,000. Villa then sold him for £200,000 to Blackburn Rovers in November 1991. Sid returned to Villa Park for a third spell on a free transfer in July 1993, staying until February 1994, when he was transferred to Derby County, from where he moved to Wolves in December of the same year. Free transfers followed to Sheffield United in December 1995, Bradford City in July 1996, Stockport County in March 1997, and finally to Burnley as reserve-team player-coach under player-manager Chris Waddle. Then in August 1998, John Gregory brought him back to Villa Park as assistant manager-coach. In a career spanning over twenty years, 'Sid' Cowans made in excess of 800 senior appearances, scoring 75 goals.

On the international stage, he played for England Youth, England Under-21 and England 'B' , and won 10 caps for the full England side, scoring twice.

Gary Shaw, *striker (40 League appearances, 18 goals; 1 appearance in the FA Cup; 3 appearances in the League Cup, 2 goals).*

Born in Castle Bromwich on 21 January 1961, Gary Shaw joined Aston Villa as an apprentice in July 1977, turning professional in January 1979 and making his league debut against Bristol City at Ashton Gate, coming on as a substitute in a 1-0 defeat on 26 August 1978. The blond striker started Villa's championship-winning season aged nineteen. He went on to make 205 first-team appearances for the Villans, in the process scoring 80 goals. In 1981 he was voted 'Young Player of the Year' by the Professional Footballer's Association, and among his other accolades was the European Cup 'Player of the Year.' He won nine caps as a Young England striker, plus seven caps for England Under-21s. His 38 league-goal partnership with Peter Withe in 1980/81 was truly memorable.

A series of knee injuries halted his career following a loan period with Blackpool in February 1988, plus brief spells on the continent with BK Copenhagen of Denmark in May 1988, and FC Klagenfurt of Austria between March and May 1989. Another short time on loan to Sheffield Wednesday later that year preceded a transfer to Walsall in February 1990, but again this didn't work out. After trying again in 1990, first at Kilmarnock, and then with Shrewsbury Town, Gary tried a last-ditch effort with Ernst Borel FC in Hong Kong. Sadly his injuries forced him to retire at the still-young age of thirty.

Peter Withe, *striker (36 League appearances, 20 goals; 1 appearance in the FA Cup; 3 appearances in the League Cup, 1 goal).*

Born in Liverpool on 30 August 1951, much-travelled striker Peter Withe had made a few appearances for Southport, Preston North End and Barrow, before trying his luck in South Africa, where he was spotted and recommended to Wolves. He joined the Molineux outfit on loan in October 1973, and then transferred officially for a bargain-basement fee of around £13,500. He made his Wolves debut in March 1974, making 12 appearances, plus three as substitute over two seasons, scoring three goals. In the summer of 1975, Peter played for Portland Timbers in the NASL, before joining Birmingham City for £50,000 in August 1975. That's where Brian Clough, not a bad judge of centre forwards, saw him and decided he would do a good job for Forest. Cloughie took him to the City Ground in September 1976 for a fee of £42,000. Withe would never have claimed to be the most skilful striker around, but his qualities of bravery and hard work more than made up for what he lacked in skill. Clough eventually sold him to Newcastle United for £200,000 in August 1978, a good profit, but was the old master too quick to cash in on his centre forward?

Peter Withe stayed in the North-East until being bought by Aston Villa in May 1980 for a transfer fee of £500,000, making his debut on 16 August 1980 against Leeds United in a 2-1 win at Elland Road. At Villa he won his second championship winners' medal to go with the one he had won with Forest in 1977/78, and of course he famously scored the winning goal for Villa in the European Cup final in 1982. In all he made 233 appearances for Villa, scoring a very creditable 92 goals.

He was capped 11 times for England between 1981 and 1984, scoring one goal, often teaming up with his former Forest strike partner Tony Woodcock. His first cap was against Brazil on 12 May 1981 in a 1-0 defeat at Wembley; his last came in the 8-0 thrashing of Turkey in the World Cup qualifying match in Istanbul on 14 November 1984, in an England team that included quite a few of his old Forest chums: Shilton, Anderson, Francis and Woodcock.

In July 1985, he moved on a free transfer to Sheffield United, then on loan to Birmingham City between September and November 1987. In July 1988 he moved to Huddersfield Town as player-coach, and subsequently back to Villa Park in January 1991, as assistant manager-coach to Josef Venglos. From there Peter tried management with Wimbledon from October 1991 to January 1992. Between 1992 and 1995, Peter was Football in the Community Officer with Port Vale before becoming Aston Villa's chief scout in 1998. He then moved to Thailand to take on the role of national team coach.

In a long and successful career, Peter Withe played in excess of 600 games and scored more than 200 goals, in the process winning two League Championships, the European Cup and the European Super Cup.

1980/81 STATISTICS

Tony Morley, *left winger (42 League appearances, 10 goals; 1 appearance in the FA Cup; 3 appearances in the League Cup, 2 goals).*

One of the fastest wingers in the game, two-footed Tony Morley provided much of the ammunition for Villa's goals, as well as netting a few in his own right.

Tony was born in Ormskirk on 26 August 1954 and signed apprentice forms for Preston North End in July 1969, turning professional in 1972. He was transferred to Burnley in February 1976, from where he joined Villa for a fee of around £200,000 in June 1979, making his debut in the 1-1 draw at Bolton Wanderers on 18 August 1979. He went on to make 180 senior appearances for Villa, scoring 34 goals, in the process helping Villa to win the League Championship, the European Cup and the European Super Cup.

In December 1983 he signed for neighbours West Bromwich Albion before moving to Japan to play for Seiko in 1985. While at Albion he was loaned out to Birmingham City for a couple of months. After a promotion-winning spell in Holland with Den Haag in 1986/87, he returned to England and played for Walsall, Notts County, West Bromwich Albion and Burnley, subsequently trying his luck with Tampa Bay Rowdies in the North American Soccer League. He later played in Malta and New Zealand before finishing his career at the age of thirty-nine with Sutton Coldfield Town at the end of season 1992/93.

Tony Morley won six full England caps, one for England 'B', also playing at Youth and Under-23 level.

David Geddis, *striker (8 League appearances, plus 1 as substitute, 4 goals; 1 substitute appearance in the Football League Cup).*

One of Ipswich Town's 1978 FA Cup-winning heroes, David Geddis was born in Carlisle on 12 March 1958. He joined Bobby Robson's Ipswich as a junior in July 1969, turning professional in August 1979, playing in Ipswich's winning FA Youth Cup side. Following a period on loan with Luton Town, he managed to establish himself at the Suffolk club during season 1977/78, when he made 26 league appearances. In 1978/79, he was restricted to 15 games and was subsequently transferred to Aston Villa in September 1979 for a fee reported to be £300,000, making his debut on 22 September 1979 in a 0-0 draw with Arsenal at Villa Park, and going on to make 56 appearances, scoring 16 goals. Villa loaned him out to Luton Town in December 1982, then sold him to Barnsley in September 1983. A year later he was transferred to Birmingham City and, following a loan spell with Brentford in September 1986, he joined Shrewsbury Town in March 1987. From the Shrews, he moved to Swindon Town in October 1988, and then to Darlington between March and May 1990. Following his retirement from the playing side of the game, he was Community Officer at Middlesbrough and, for a time, reserve-team coach.

On the international scene, he played for England 'B' and the England Youth teams.

1980/81 Statistics

Summary of League Appearances:

42 – Jimmy Rimmer, Kenny Swain, Ken McNaught, Dennis Mortimer, Des Bremner, Gordon Cowans, Tony Morley.

40 – Gary Shaw.

39 – Allan Evans.

36 – Peter Withe.

21 – Gary Williams.

19 – Colin Gibson.

8 – David Geddis.

5 – Eamonn Deacy.

Substitute Appearances:

4 – Eamonn Deacy.

2 – Colin Gibson.

1 – Gary Williams, David Geddis.

The League Goalscorers:

20 – Peter Withe.

18 – Gary Shaw.

10 – Tony Morley.

8 – Allan Evans.

5 – Gordon Cowans (4 penalites).

4 – David Geddis.

3 – Dennis Mortimer.

2 – Des Bremner.

2 – Own goals.

Villa scored a total of 72 league goals and conceded 40 goals.

Summary of Appearances in the League Cup:

3 – Jimmy Rimmer, Kenny Swain, Colin Gibson, Allan Evans, Ken McNaught, Dennis Mortimer, Des Bremner, Peter Withe, Gordon Cowans, Tony Morley.

2 – Gary Shaw.

1 – David Geddis.

Substitute appearances:

1 – Eamonn Deacy, Gary Shaw.

Goalscorers in the League Cup:

2 – Tony Morley, Gary Shaw.

1 – Peter Withe.

Villa scored 5 goals in their three League Cup ties and conceded 3.

Summary of FA Cup Appearances:

1 – Jimmy Rimmer, Kenny Swain, Gary Williams, Allan Evans, Ken McNaught, Dennis Mortimer, Des Bremner, Gary Shaw, Peter Withe, Gordon Cowans, Tony Morley.

Substitute appearances:

1 – David Geddis.

Villa didn't manage to score a goal in the FA Cup, and conceded 1 in this competition.

1980/81 STATISTICS

The Backroom Staff:

Ron Saunders, *Manager*

Known as one of football's hard men, Ron Saunders was born in Birkenhead on 6 November 1932, joining Everton as a junior in 1948 before turning professional in February 1951. Ron was an old-fashioned centre forward, strong and determined with a powerful shot. Things didn't work out for him at Everton, so in 1956 he tried his luck down south with Tonbridge, where his no-nonsense style brought him to the attention of Gillingham, who bought him in 1957. An £8,000 move to First Division Portsmouth in September 1958 was spoiled when Pompey were relegated at the end of that season. They finished third from bottom of the Second Division the season after, and were relegated to the Third Division at the end of the 1960/61 campaign. Ron's goals helped Portsmouth win the Third Division championship in 1961/62 and consolidate their position as a mid-table Second Division side. He moved to Watford just after the start of the 1964/65 season, and then to Charlton Athletic a year later, where he ended his playing career.

Ron Saunders' career in football management started at Yeovil Town in May 1967, followed by a short spell in charge of Oxford United in 1969. He was appointed manager of Norwich City in July 1969, and stayed until November 1973, winning the Second Division championship in 1971/72, and guiding them to runners-up in the 1973 League Cup, before taking up a lucrative offer to manage Manchester City, where he stayed until April 1974, again reaching the League Cup final only to lose 2-1 to Wolves at Wembley.

Ron brought his brand of stern discipline to Aston Villa in June 1974, gaining promotion to the First Division from a second-place finish in his first season and winning the League Cup in 1974/75, beating his old club Norwich City 1-0 in the final. Villa won the League Cup again in 1976/77, beating his first club Everton 3-2 in the second replay at Old Trafford. The first game had ended 0-0 at Wembley and the Hillsborough replay finished 1-1 after extra time.

In 1980/81, Ron's finest hour came when he steered Villa to the league championship. But instead of being left to continue his trophy laden time at Villa Park, amid a background of animosity and disillusionment he left the club in February 1982 before he could watch 'his team' win the European Cup in 1981/82 and the European Super Cup in 1982. The 1981/82 season hadn't been going as well as Villa would have liked. Injuries to key players were finally catching up with the squad and the absence of Gary Shaw and his goals, coupled with an unsettled team line-up, took its toll on confidence. Dismissal from the League Cup on 20 January by West Bromwich Albion, and being knocked out in the fifth round of the FA Cup at Tottenham on 13 February, added to the three defeats and two draws in the six league games since the New Year, did nothing to improve things. When he joined Villa, Ron Saunders was given a six-year contract, time enough to produce a winning team, which of course he did. This was subsequently changed to a three-year rolling contract, to which Ron said he was now worse off than when he started.

Much to the consternation of Villa fans, in February 1982, Ron moved across the city to take up the post of manager of Birmingham City. He stayed at St Andrews until January 1986, during which time the Blues were relegated to the Second Division at the end of the 1983/84 season, before gaining promotion in 1984/85. Again, after only one season back in the top flight, Birmingham were relegated along with West Bromwich Albion in 1985/86, Ron having left in January 1986 to take over the manager's role at the Albion, where he famously told Steve Bull that he would never be a top goalscorer. In September 1987, Ron Saunders decided to pack it in. I guess we'll never know if he could have taken his Aston Villa side to even more success had he not left when he did. Many thought him a dour advocate of negative football, and he certainly didn't appear to cultivate a popular image with the media or the fans, but without doubt he was one of Villa's most successful post-war managers. The increased weight of the Aston Villa trophy cabinet surely testifies to the veracity of this.

Tony Barton, *Assistant Manager*

Tony Barton was born in Sutton, Surrey on 8 April 1937, and joined Fulham as a junior in June 1953, turning professional in May 1954. Tony was an old-fashioned right winger, who played for England at Schoolboy and Youth level. After five years at Craven Cottage, in which time he made 51 league appearances scoring eight goals, in December 1959 he moved to Nottingham Forest, playing in 22 league games, scoring one goal. He was transferred to Portsmouth in December 1961. From then until 1967 he made 129 league appearances, plus one as substitute, scoring 34 goals. He subsequently accepted a post on the coaching staff at Fratton Park, before eventually linking up with Ron Saunders at Villa Park as coach and assistant manager.

When Saunders resigned as manager in February 1982, Tony Barton stepped into his shoes (he didn't get Ron's company Mercedes) and, of course, led Aston Villa to their momentous 1-0 victory over Bayern Munich to win the coveted European Cup on 26 May 1982 in Rotterdam. The triumph quelled the disappointment of an eleventh-place finish in the league in season 1981/82 after the euphoria of the previous season. Tony managed to get Villa up into fifth place in the league the following season, winning the European Super Cup in January by beating Barcelona, but losing the semi-final of the European Cup to Juventus was a bitter pill to swallow. Tony Barton was sacked in May 1984, following the 1983/84 season, when Villa slumped to tenth place in the league and had lost to Everton in the Milk Cup semi-final as well as being dumped out of the FA Cup and the UEFA Cup.

He moved to Fourth Division Northampton Town for one season, 1984/85, but finished second from bottom of the league, suffering a heart attack during his time there. In September 1985 Chris Nicholl hired Tony as his assistant-manager at Southampton, where he stayed until May 1988, returning to Portsmouth as assistant manager to Alan Ball, then becoming caretaker manager until 1991. He ended his career scouting for several clubs including Southampton and Bournemouth.

Sadly, Tony died at the young age of fifty-six, on 20 August 1993, following a second heart attack.

Champions Villa arrive at the town hall on an open-topped bus.

Other titles published by Tempus
Aston Villa Football Club
TONY MATTHEWS

From their founding by members of the Weslyan chapel cricket team in the 1870s, Aston Villa have gone from strength to strength. This book illustrates the Villans' history and includes many great achievements, such as the winning of the double in 1897 and the lifting of the European Cup in the 1980s. This collection of more than 200 photographs, programme covers and cartoons represents some of the important pictorial records of this great club and is an essential read for anyone with an interest in Aston Villa.

0 7524 3123 4

West Midlands Football
TONY MATTHEWS

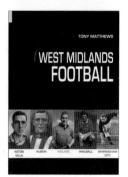

Focusing on five clubs – Aston Villa, Birmingham City, West Bromwich Albion, Wolverhampton Wanderers and Walsall – this is the story of League and cup football in the West Midlands. This part of England has seen no small amount of footballing success, with League Championships, FA Cups, League Cups and European honours being won by West Midlands clubs. The great players and passionately fought local derbies are recounted in a fine illustrated history that is sure to delight all fans.

0 7524 3270 2

If you are interested in purchasing other books published by Tempus, or in case you have difficulty finding any Tempus books in your local bookshop, you can also place orders directly through our website

www.tempus-publishing.com